WILLIAM JAMES
and a Science of Religions

COLUMBIA SERIES IN SCIENCE AND RELIGION

The Columbia Series in Science and Religion is sponsored by the Center for the Study of Science and Religion (CSSR) at Columbia University. It is a forum for the examination of issues that lie at the boundary of these two complementary ways of comprehending the world and our place in it. By examining the intersections between one or more of the sciences and one or more religions, the CSSR hopes to stimulate dialogue and encourage understanding.

ROBERT POLLACK
The Faith of Biology and the Biology of Faith

ALAN WALLACE, ED.
Buddhism and Science: Breaking New Ground

LISA SIDERIS
*Environmental Ethics, Ecological Theory, and Natural Selection:
Suffering and Responsibility*

WILLIAM JAMES
and a Science of Religions

Reexperiencing
The Varieties of Religious Experience

Wayne Proudfoot, *editor*

COLUMBIA UNIVERSITY PRESS

New York

Columbia University Press
Publishers Since 1893
New York Chichester, West Sussex
Copyright © 2004 Columbia University Press

Library of Congress Cataloging-in-Publication Data
William James and a science of religions : reexperiencing The varieties of religious experience / Wayne Proudfoot, editor.
p. cm. — (Columbia series in science and religion)
Includes bibliographical references.
ISBN 0-231-13204-2
1. James, William, 1842-1910. Varieties of religious experience.   2. Experience (Religion).   3. Psychology, Religious.   4. Religion.   5. Conversion. I. Proudfoot, Wayne, 1939– I. Series.
BL53.J363W55   2004
204'.2—dc22   2003063537

Columbia University Press books are printed on
permanent and durable acid-free paper.

Printed in the United States of America

c 10 9 8 7 6 5 4 3 2 1

Contents

Contributors

Jerome Bruner is University Professor at New York University.

David A. Hollinger is Preston Hotchkis Professor of American History at the University of California, Berkeley.

Philip Kitcher is John Dewey Professor of Philosophy at Columbia University.

Wayne Proudfoot is Professor of Religion at Columbia University.

Richard Rorty is Professor of Comparative Literature at Stanford University.

Ann Taves is Professor of the History of Christianity and American Religion at the Claremont School of Theology and Professor of Religion at Claremont Graduate University.

WILLIAM JAMES
and a Science of Religions

Introduction

A century after its publication, *The Varieties of Religious Experience* continues to be widely read, but it has not yet received the critical attention it deserves. In recent years philosophers, historians, and scholars of literature and religion have shown renewed interest in American pragmatism and in the writings of William James. He is now read not only for historical reasons but also for insights that might illumine contemporary discussion in each of these disciplines. With few exceptions, however, scholars interested in James's pragmatism, his work in psychology, or his historical or literary influence have not turned their attention to *Varieties*, and those in religion have neglected it as well.

Varieties occupies an important place in the development of James's pragmatism. "Pragmatism" was first used publicly as the name for a distinctive approach to philosophical analysis in his 1898 lecture at Berkeley, "Philosophical Conceptions and Practical Results."[1] There James paraphrased and revised Charles Sanders Peirce's criterion for explicating the meaning of a term by attention to the practical effects one expects from the use of the term.[2] Scholars have noted that passages from the lecture are included in James's *Pragmatism* of 1907. But they have not noted that passages from the Berkeley talk are also included in *Varieties*, and that James described it as a rehearsal for the Gifford Lectures in Edinburgh, which were to be published as that book. At crucial points in *Varieties*, including the introductory chapter, the lecture on philosophy, and the conclusion, he employs his new pragmatic theory of inquiry.

In the Berkeley lecture, James introduces his pragmatic approach, gratefully acknowledging Peirce as progenitor, and then uses it to clarify what is at stake in the debate between theism and materialism. To determine the meaning of the idea of God, he says, and to bring out the real differences in the debate, one ought to consider actual religious experiences and their practical consequences for people's lives. *Varieties* is a study of these experiences and consequences, and it is the first step toward implementation of the approach to the philosophy of religion that James had advocated at Berkeley. Five years after the publication of *Varieties,* James opens *Pragmatism* with the hope that his new philosophy will satisfy religious demands as well as those of hard-headed empiricism. That book culminates with a chapter on pragmatism and religion. Religion thus figures prominently in James's two most explicit and most important statements of his pragmatism.

The application to religion is not fortuitous. For more than twenty years preceding the Berkeley lecture, James had been reflecting on Peirce's theory of inquiry and its implications for assessing religious belief.[3] In *Varieties* he proposes that traditional philosophy of religion be replaced by a "science of religions." Such a science would study religious beliefs, experiences, and practices, "confronting the spontaneous religious constructions with the results of natural science," and arrive at some possible conceptions that might be tested by considering the consequences of living by them.[4] James says that he doesn't see why a critical science of religions of this sort might not eventually command as much respect as a physical science, and he hopes that *Varieties* will be a small contribution to it.

James was critical of the identification of science with materialism, but not of science itself. When published in 1890, his textbook *The Principles of Psychology* was widely regarded as the leader in the field. That book ranged from considering the most recent German experiments on reaction time and on memory to phenomenological description and philosophical reflection. Peirce's article containing his pragmatic criterion of meaning was one of a series collectively titled "Illustrations of the Logic of Science." The idea of inquiry is central to pragmatism, which was modeled initially on scientific inquiry. Peirce, James, and John Dewey each argued that no inquiry is without presuppositions and interests, that the questions that elicit inquiry set constraints on acceptable answers, and that beliefs are always assessed under conditions of uncertainty. Ordinary inquiry does not differ in these respects from scientific inquiry. Differences arise only through the ways in which scientists discipline inquiry and institutionalize it.

The recent revival of interest in pragmatism stems largely from Richard Rorty's *Philosophy and the Mirror of Nature* (1979), in which he stressed the ubiquity of interpretation in inquiry. His subsequent articles illustrated this chiefly with examples taken from the humanities and the interpretation of texts. As a result, the connection between pragmatism and scientific inquiry was deemphasized, and pragmatism has had almost as much influence in departments of literature and culture as it has in departments of philosophy. But it is important to remember that Peirce, James, and the classical pragmatists began with an interest in science, and in the relation of scientific inquiry to ordinary inquiry.

In the preface to *Varieties,* James writes that he had originally planned to divide his lectures into two parts, the first a descriptive survey of religious appetites and the second a philosophical reflection on them. The descriptive part, he says, expanded to include the whole series, and he was forced to confine his philosophical suggestions to a few pages in the conclusion and the postscript. Misled by this disclaimer and by James's frequent quotations from fresh and lively descriptions of personal experiences, some readers may have viewed the book in this way. But it is not simply descriptive. From his opening distinction between descriptive and explanatory judgments on the one hand, and evaluative judgments on the other, to the conclusion and postscript, James proposes criteria, constructs working definitions and typologies, suggests and weighs explanatory hypotheses, and evaluates religious beliefs and practices. He proposes a new way of practicing the philosophy of religion, of which he takes this book to be an example. As David Hollinger shows in the first essay, *Varieties* is part of a lifelong project to consider how religious questions could be adjudicated, with particular attention to the relation between religion and science.

The authors of the essays in this volume take James's project and his proposals seriously, and consider their value for current discussions about the best ways to describe, explain, and evaluate religious beliefs, practices, and institutions. Each picks up a theme running through the book and suggests how James's treatment of that theme can fruitfully be brought to bear, sometimes with revisions or extensions, on current debates.

David Hollinger places *Varieties* within James's continuing reflection on how to resolve the tension between the legacy of Protestant Christianity and the demands of science. Hollinger shows that *Varieties* is a transitional work situated between two different strategies James uses to defend the beliefs and culture of liberal Protestantism against critics who argued that the methods and successes of scientific inquiry posed a challenge to religious belief. The first strategy, developed through the 1880s and much of the 1890s, is exhibited in *The Will to Believe*, and especially in the title essay. That strategy was to separate religious claims and ways of adjudicating them from those of science. In the second strategy, articulated most fully in *Pragmatism* of 1907, James affirms an epistemic unity in which all concepts and beliefs are products of previous inquiry and are subject to revision in the light of new doubts, new evidence, or new purposes. The "science of religions" James proposes in *Varieties* removes religion from the private sphere and brings it out in the open for public scrutiny and evaluation. Hollinger looks carefully at each of these works, showing how awareness of this shift in strategies enables a more accurate reading of them, as well as a better understanding of James's views on religion.

Hollinger provides a close reading of James's descriptions of experiences and of forms of saintliness in *Varieties* in order to show that the liberal Protestantism James defends is culturally quite specific, arising out of the tradition of Protestant dissenters. James criticizes Catholic forms of piety throughout, dismissing them as extreme and preferring a different kind of asceticism. The general terms in which he couches his judgments can mask the specificity of the forms of belief and practice that he criticizes and recommends.

In *Varieties* James writes that religion, characterized in the broadest possible terms, consists of the belief that there is an unseen order, and that our supreme good lies in adjusting ourselves to it.[5] Wayne Proudfoot argues that this question of an unseen order occupied James throughout his writings on religion. In the Berkeley lecture he applied Peirce's pragmatic criterion to the term "God" and found it equivalent to belief in an eternal moral order. This, he said, is what is at stake in debates between theism and materialism. In *Varieties* James repeatedly compares and considers the relation between religious and naturalistic views of the world.

Proudfoot distinguishes between two lines in James's narrative. In one the question of the causal explanation of an experience is irrelevant to a judgment about its religious significance. In the other James is preoccupied with the question of naturalism and with the issue of whether naturalistic explanations of religious experiences are sufficient. The first line is the dominant one, and is stated explicitly by James both at the outset and in several important places throughout the text. But the second line is present as well, and much of the intellectual energy of the book is focused upon it.

Proudfoot observes that a striking difference between *Varieties* and contemporary studies of religion is James's inattention to historical context. James does not consider historical explanations either of the experiences he examines or of the unseen order that figures so prominently in his conception of religion. Proudfoot suggests that a historical naturalism would allow for this order to be brought into a realm that would permit inquiry about its character, its causes, its consequences, and even how it might be altered.

Ann Taves examines in detail the psychological findings and theories that James drew on in *Varieties*, and argues that the use he made of them constitutes an important contribution toward a theory of religion. In *Varieties* and elsewhere James refers to the discovery of consciousness existing beyond the ordinary field, or extramarginal consciousness, as the most important step forward in psychology since he had been a student of the subject. Taves distinguishes between different kinds of extramarginal consciousness for which claims were made in the contemporary psychological literature, and between different theories to account for them. The French psychologist Pierre Janet regarded all manifestations of a "secondary self" as pathological, while James's friend Frederick Myers argued that this subliminal consciousness also occurs in normal subjects. Taves shows how James uses these findings and theories to compare religious experiences with such nonreligious mental phenomena as hallucinations, hypnotism, automatism, double personality, and mediumship. James could compare religious with nonreligious phenomena, explain both in terms of subliminal consciousness, and still leave open all questions of ultimate origins, which he took to lie outside of the purview of a science of religions. Building on Myers, James placed the pathological, the normal, and the potentially supernormal within a common frame of reference. Taves argues that James's method in *Varieties*, the theory he sets forth, and his neutrality about questions of origin are important for the current scientific study of religion.

While Taves reads *Varieties* in the light of James's contemporaries, Jerome Bruner considers his legacy for twentieth-century psychology and theories of culture. He offers some personal reflections on James's influence on the cognitive revolution in psychology. As one of the chief architects of that revolution, Bruner is well placed to consider this influence. He reminisces about his experience as a graduate student in psychology at Harvard during the forties, in a department dominated by behaviorism. He and some of his fellow students read *The Principles of Psychology* and *Varieties* largely outside the classroom. Bruner writes that the attention they brought to the role of the mind in knowing and acting was, in part, a result of the influence of James.

Bruner suggests that the turn to the cognitive throughout the social sciences, in the anthropology of Edward Evans-Pritchard and Clifford Geertz, for instance, and in the work of the historian and philosopher Michel Foucault, is a natural adjunct to James's pragmatism, even in the absence of direct influence. He notes that James attends throughout *Varieties* to how religious realities are constructed. "The gods we stand by are the gods we need and can use," James writes, "whose demands on us are reinforcements of our demands on ourselves and on one another." James shows that religious experiences are shaped by aesthetic preferences as well as by such ritual practices as auricular confession and prayer. In this regard, he anticipates a central occupation of much twentieth-century cognitive psychology and cultural anthropology.

Richard Rorty argues that James is inconsistent in *Varieties* about whether he is presenting experiential evidence for supernaturalism or arguing that religious belief and experience are good for people and that they have a right to those beliefs. This shows in ambiguous uses of both "religion" and "experience." James sometimes writes as if a religious view of the world were opposed to a naturalistic one, but at other times he uses "religious" to refer to a quality of experience that is not at all incompatible with naturalism. Rorty thinks this much more consistent with his pragmatism.

James's ambiguous use of "religious" is matched by a similar ambiguity in his use of "experience." It is unclear in *Varieties* whether or not James subscribes to the "myth of the given." On one reading he seems to think that religious experience provides evidence that bears on the truth of theism. On another, his view of experience appears closer to that of Wittgenstein or Sellars, and his chief argument in the book is that religious experiences have good consequences for life. Pragmatism, Rorty writes, leads to the second of these options, but James has metaphysical interests that go beyond his pragmatism. Rorty thinks that we would be well advised to take the pragmatism and leave the metaphysics.

Philip Kitcher considers, and rejects, what he calls the natural reading of *Varieties* as an argument for the validity of religious experience, and the simple pragmatic reading as an argument that religious experiences are expedient or beneficial for those who have them. Neither of these arguments, he thinks, can easily be ascribed to someone of James's intelligence and sophistication.

For a more plausible reading, Kitcher goes back to James's 1896 essay entitled "The Will to Believe." James and William Clifford, his chief target in that essay, agree that there can be no such thing as religious knowledge. But James successfully rebuts Clifford's claim that it is "wrong, always, everywhere and for anyone, to believe anything upon insufficient evidence." He shows that religious belief responds to important aspects of human life, and that it can bring about positive changes in people's lives. Kitcher considers Clifford's objection and James's response, arguing that the essay points toward a proper way to assess religious belief and practice. James continues and deepens that assessment in *Varieties*, where he looks at systemic effects of religious beliefs and practices in order to evaluate them more adequately on consequentialist grounds. Kitcher's previous work on the evaluation of methods and topics of research in the sciences affords a perspective from which he can appreciate and begin to extend James's project in *Varieties*.

Taken together, these essays bring different perspectives to bear on the place of *Varieties* in the development of James's pragmatism, and on his views of the relations between religion and science. Both are important issues for the understanding of James's thought and of its contribution to current debates.

These papers were written for a colloquium on the centennial of William James's *The Varieties of Religious Experience* held at Columbia University on March 24 and 25, 2002. The colloquium was sponsored by the John Templeton Foundation and was held under the auspices of the Center for the Study of Science and Religion at Columbia. Special thanks are due to Professor Robert Pollack, director of the center, and to Andrea Villanti of the center's staff.

A version of Ann Taves's article in this volume was delivered as the 2002 William James Lecture on Religious Experience at Harvard Divinity School and published as "Religious Experience and the Divisible Self: William James (and Frederick Myers) as Theorist(s) of Religion," in *Journal of the American Academy of Religion* 71, 2 (March 2003): 303–326.

NOTES

1. William James, *Pragmatism* (Cambridge: Harvard University Press, 1985), 257–270.

2. Peirce wrote that a term could be clarified by considering the practical effects one might expect from its object. To say that something is "hard" is to say that it cannot easily be scratched. James broadened Peirce's suggestion to include effects that do not require prior action. Charles Sanders Peirce, "How to Make Our Ideas Clear," in *The Essential Peirce: Selected Philosophical Writings, Vol.1 1867–1893*, ed. Nathan Houser and Christian Kloesel (Bloomington: Indiana University Press, 1992), 124–141; James, *Pragmatism*, 259.

3. See his articles collected in *The Will to Believe* (Cambridge: Harvard University Press, 1979). This volume is dedicated to Peirce.

4. William James, *The Varieties of Religious Experience* (Cambridge: Harvard University Press, 1985), 359–360. See also James, *The Will to Believe*, 8–9.

5. James, *Varieties*, 51.

1

∞

"Damned for God's Glory"

William James and the Scientific Vindication
of Protestant Culture

DAVID A. HOLLINGER

When William James died in 1910, his lifelong friend, Supreme Court Justice Oliver Wendell Holmes Jr., remarked that when James dealt with religion, he had tried "to turn the lights down low so as to give miracle a chance."[1] Many items in the James canon feed this suspicion. Yet *The Varieties of Religious Experience*, James's most sustained treatment of religion, constitutes a proposal that even the most private, mystical experiences offered as evidence for religious belief be brought out into the open, be made, indeed, the primary subject matter for "a science of religions," an empirically oriented, publicly warranted inquiry that James envisaged as a successor discipline to "philosophy of religion."[2]

These two potentially contradictory starting points—James's self-presentation in his greatest contribution to religious studies and Holmes's skepticism toward that self-presentation—can remind us of an enduring tension at the center of James's intellectual life. The tension is between the demands of the inherited culture of Protestant Christianity,

9

with its belief in a supernatural God potentially responsive to human striving, and the demands of modern science, with its emphasis on the intersubjective testing of claims based on the data of the senses. That James was much troubled by the apparent conflict between these demands is not a matter of dispute. It is rightly taken for granted by virtually all James scholars, even by those who find this bit of history to be a philosophically irrelevant distraction. What is not taken for granted, even by those who find James's religious preoccupations pertinent today, is any particular understanding of the life project that this science-religion tension generated in James. Nor do James scholars agree upon just what relation *Varieties* has to James's other work. Claims about the continuity between "The Will to Believe" and *Varieties*, for example, are rarely engaged critically because many of the philosophers who address "The Will to Believe" are not much interested in *Varieties*, and many of the religious studies scholars for whom *Varieties* is a vital text have relatively little invested in the agendas that drive philosophers' interpretation of "The Will to Believe."

I want to begin by calling attention to just how the science-religion issue is displayed in *Varieties*. I will then locate *Varieties* chronologically and logically in what I believe it is fair to describe as James's career-long defense of certain central aspects of the culture of liberal Protestantism as understood and cherished by many educated Americans of his generation. This is the life project from which we today are tempted to detach James's ideas. Specifically, I will interpret *Varieties* as a product of the particular phase in James's career when he was shifting from one strategy to another in that defense. Before I proceed to the text, let me indicate telegraphically what those two strategies were, and allude to a third strategy popular in his milieu that James was concerned to discredit.

The first strategy was a highly sophisticated version of the classic "separate spheres" doctrine, an effort to protect Protestantism from science by marking off a distinct category of beliefs that science could not be expected to touch. The second strategy was to embrace in a Peircean mode the epistemic unity of all experience and belief, and to vindicate the generic human ideals for which Protestantism was a historic vehicle within rather than outside the discursive constraints of modern science, once those constraints were properly understood. When he wrote *Varieties* in 1902, James had recently drawn away from the first of these strategies, which he had developed most fully in "The Will to Believe" in 1897, but he was not yet confident about the second, Peircean strategy, which he later employed in 1907 in the book entitled *Pragmatism*. In *Varieties* James was still trying to figure out how best to carry out the second strategy, and he was also trying to decide just what it was that he wanted to vindicate scientifically under the sign of "religion." And while he was working out this transition from one strategy to another, he remained preoccupied with the enormous appeal to his audience of a third strategy, that of absolute idealism. It is too easy today to underestimate that appeal. The absolute idealist Josiah Royce, James's Harvard colleague, was a dialectician so formidable that he was then known, after the reigning heavyweight champion, as the John L. Sullivan of philosophy. By contrast, James was a psychologist trying to do philosophy and, in the view of many philosophers, failing.

But I will return to all of that. Now to *Varieties* itself, and the specific form that the science-religion tension takes within that text.

James's ostensibly specieswide account of religious experience is deeply Protestant in structure, tone, and implicit theology. Even the categories of religious experience around which *Varieties* is organized, and the order in which James describes them, have this quality. As theologian Richard R. Niebuhr and others have pointed out, James, by moving from "healthy-mindedness" to the "sick soul" to the "divided self" to "conversion" and then to "saintliness," follows the prescribed sequence of the evangelical Protestant conversion narrative.[3] Although James presents his subject matter as generically human, and says explicitly several times that Buddhism, Islam, and Judaism as well as Christianity have been settings for religious experiences the essence of which he seeks to confront, the frequency and character of his use of Protestant examples tells us much about what was at stake for himself.

James takes the first of his many extended quotations from the writings of the seventeenth-century English Quaker, George Fox. This is an interesting choice to represent the radical alterity of religious experience, as the realm James suggests is so foreign to his enlightened, modern listeners at Edinburgh and to his similarly enlightened and modern readers generally. Fox's state of mind, which James denotes as "pathological," was indeed bizarre in contrast with that expressed by the average Anglican, Presbyterian, or Unitarian of 1902. But Fox's piety was that of highly familiar dissenting English Protestantism. Fox was marginal, all right, but what he was marginal to was mainstream: the Anglo-American Protestant tradition as comprehended by James's audience. And the sensibility of which Fox was an extreme case was the widely approved sensibility of Puritan-Quaker humility. In introducing Fox's testimony, moreover, James observes that he brought to England a Christianity closer to that of the original gospel than England had ever seen. James describes it as "a religion of veracity," an interesting construction in a science-and-religion milieu in which the agnostic T. H. Huxley was often quoted for praising science as "fanaticism for veracity."[4] James keeps going back to Fox, and cites him another nine times at various points in the book.

One of the places in which James reverts to Fox is in his pivotal discussion of saintliness, which, as John E. Smith reminds us in his introduction to the now-standard Harvard edition of *Varieties*, is the critical core of James's effort to justify religion on the basis of its results.[5] But the Protestant orientation of James's discussion of saintliness is much more pronounced than many commentators have noted. To a very large extent, these chapters on saintliness amount to a celebration of the strict observance of exactly the personal morality prescribed historically by dissenting Protestants in Britain and America. When James comes to talk about the behavioral manifestations of successful conversion, he moves quickly into a discussion of "reformed drunkards" and of males cured of "sexual temptation." This then leads to a footnote about a woman who, under the inspiration of religious experience, was able finally to quit smoking.[6] In James's two chapters on saintliness, we find ourselves right in the middle of the culture explored by James's contemporary Harold Frederic in *The Damnation of Theron Ware*, and affectionately chuckled at in our own time by Garrison Keillor.

Asceticism and charity are the two virtues on which James spends the most time in his account of saintliness, but a striking theme in his examples of charity is that of self-humbling on the part of the giver, as though the point was not so much to enhance the circumstances of the beneficiary as to diminish pride of self in the benefactor. Among James's examples are Francis of Assisi and Ignatius Loyola, both of whom he mentions for having "exchanged their garments with those of filthy beggars."[7]

Here the distinction between James's Catholic and Protestant examples becomes revealing. James refers repeatedly to the ways in which the Roman church has more or less specialized in ascetic piety. But as he alternates between Catholic and Protestant cases, a pattern emerges. After two quite benign testimonies from a Unitarian and a Methodist telling of the taking up of humble clothing and the refusing of rich food, James cites a French country priest who would never drink when thirsty and never take cover against the cold. Then James gives us Cotton Mather of Massachusetts, displaying virtuous asceticism by merely refusing to touch his beloved wife's body in her last moments of life in order that he might humbly accept her passage into God's hands. This is one of James's most gentle, attractive examples of self-abnegation, the release of a loved one. But suddenly James presents St. John of the Cross, the sixteenth-century Spanish mystic who advocated the despising of oneself, the yearning that others will despise you, and the turning of one's soul toward whatever is disgusting and contemptible. This case then slides into another Catholic example, the fourteenth-century German mystic Suso, whose account of his own physical self-mortification—sleeping on a bed of nails and the like—is one of the longest single quotations in the whole of *Varieties*. James breaks off this flagrantly masochistic and some would say mildly pornographic quotation by saying that he will "spare" us the further "recital of poor Suso's self-inflicted tortures."[8]

Several pages later James asks his readers if he might have left an impression "of extravagance." And sure enough, he then allows that while there is much to admire in these saintly lives, he is not urging that they be "imitated." Then he launches into a vigorous critique of what he calls "excess" in "saintly virtue." The freethinkers, James admits, are on to something when they complain of certain unhealthy tendencies among the more fanatical of religious believers. Their mentality is "too one-sided to be admirable," he declares, and then provides a long quotation from a Catholic saint who James says has renounced all human uses for her asceticism. James then turns to St. Teresa, for whom he says he can feel only "pity that so much vitality of soul should have found such poor employment." This is then followed by a whole string of Catholic testimonies, including one from St. Louis of Gonzaga, whom James actually calls "repulsive." Such cases "in the annals of Catholic saintship," he says explicitly, "make us rub our Protestant eyes."[9] There is no question who the "we" or the "us" is whenever James invokes these portentous pronouns.

What casts James's treatment of Fox and other canonical Protestants into bold relief, then, is not so much his fleeting use of Muslim and Jewish cases but the sustained treatment he gives to Catholics. One can easily get the impression that *Varieties* is a noninvidious harvest of the most intense spiritual moments of all the major religions, especially of Christianity, embracing Catholic as well as Protestant variations. But no. *Varieties* is constructed to foreground certain religious sensibilities and not others, and to present the core of religion in general as having been most attractively manifest in exactly the cultural tradition to which James's listeners and readers were directly heir. Too often, the so-called descriptive chapters of *Varieties* are read as a rather indiscriminate reportage of random and widely dispersed "raw materials" punctuated by James's respectful commentary. But if instead we read these chapters as literary texts, with attention to his selection of quotations and their dynamic relation to one another, we gain greater access to James's center of religious gravity.

That James was being judgmental when he talked about saintliness cannot be emphasized enough, given the tendency of some readers to take the bulk of *Varieties* as merely descriptive. "We must judge," James says, and we must do so "not sentimentally," but "by our own intellectual standards." He then quotes Nietzsche's attack on saintliness as being overdrawn, but properly skeptical. Right in the middle of this discussion, James says that a goal of the science of religions is "to test saintliness by common sense, to use human standards to help us decide how far the religious life commends itself as an ideal kind of human activity." These standards, he is quick to explain, are historically specific and are grounded in a process of cultural "evolution." "What with science, idealism, and democracy, our own imagination has grown to need a God of an entirely different temperament" from that of the Catholic saints.[10]

James's frank acceptance of the idea that our gods are constructed socially on the basis of our historical experience shows just how liberal was the Protestantism with which he was comfortable. "The gods we stand by are the gods we need and can use, the gods whose demands on us are reinforcements of our demands on our ourselves, and on one another." It is for us, then, said James about himself and his contemporaries, to apply to "religious beliefs" a kind of critical selection analogous to natural selection; we are engaged in "the survival of the humanly fittest" and the "elimination of the humanly unfit" religious beliefs.[11] No wonder James's funeral sermon was preached by George A. Gordon, the Congregationalist minister then known as "the Matterhorn of the Protestant Alps," who understood that religious evolution from antiquity onward had been leading up to his church in the heart of Boston.[12]

James's evolutionary language concerning the survival of the fittest religions under modern scrutiny can turn us from the aspects of *Varieties* that reveal its firm foundation in liberal Protestantism to those aspects that indicate more fully the shape and scope of the "science of religions" that James sought to establish. These elements of *Varieties* display his sense of the scientific side of the tension that drives the work.

James defines his science of religions the most sharply against what he calls "dogmatic theology" and more generally against "philosophy of religion," the alleged character of which he conveys with quotations from such idealist metaphysicians as Josiah Royce and James Caird, and various scholastic thinkers, including Cardinal Newman. Against the propensity of this class of thinkers for "metaphysics and deduction," James calls for "criticism and induction," and for the testing of religious ideas in their capacity as hypotheses, a favorite word that he italicizes in his most rigorously formulated account of what makes his science of religions different from what philosophers and theologians have done with religion in the past.[13]

Central to James's science of religion are the ideals of intersubjective testability and consensus. The severity of his presentation of these ideals is one of the least appreciated themes of *Varieties*. Although the experiences he wants scrutinized are private in origin, the idea is now to consider them in a public frame, to bring them within the scope of disciplined, empirical inquiry. The result will be a scientific distillation and evaluation of religious experience. James stresses that any philosophically sound view of life needs to take into account the totality of human experience. It was science's breadth of scope, science's ability to confront the particulars of individual experience with that of thousands and millions of other human individuals, that gave it the opportunity to build such a philosophically sound view of life. Religious claims to truth need to be integrated with our body of truths. "By confronting spontaneous religious constructions with the results of natural science," insists James, we can "eliminate doctrines that are now known to be scientifically absurd or incongruous." Our science "can offer mediation between different believers, and help bring about consensus of opinion."[14]

James is so attracted to the ideal of scholarly consensus that he uses the failure of the idealists to achieve it as a sign of the obvious inadequacy of their ideas. This is a stunning move on the part of James, who had been for so long a polemical defender of idiosyncratic minorities against the apparent tyrannies of learned majorities. And he seems to sense how remarkable a move it is, because he accompanies it with a long and defensive footnote apologizing for not even trying to meet with arguments the claims of Royce and the other metaphysical idealists.[15] He knows how odd it is of him to dismiss someone on the grounds that his or her claims have failed to win over the leaders of a professional community.

I have been quoting from the chapter entitled "Philosophy," but James picks up the same themes in his final chapter, "Conclusions." There he hits hard his determination that the results of religious experience be squared with the results of the rest of experience: it is among "the duties of the science of religions," he declares, "to keep religion in connexion with the rest of Science," with the word "science" capitalized, and not ironically as James had been inclined to do in earlier years. Even in the "Postscript," that enigmatic and disjointed indicator of the depth and texture of James's nervousness about the signals sent in the Gifford Lectures, James returns to "legitimate requirements" that must be met by any hypothesis.[16]

And it is those requirements that James believes are not met by the people he calls "medical materialists" in the first chapter of *Varieties*, entitled "Religion and Neurology." There, he goes after the reductionists who dismiss Saul's transformation into Paul on the road to Damascus as an epileptic seizure, and who treat "George Fox's discontents with the shams of his age, and his pining for spiritual veracity" as symptoms of "a disordered colon." But he most adamantly condemns these cultured despisers of religion on the basis of strictly uniformitarian, scientific principles. It is the failure of the reductionists to be consistent materialists that most gives the lie to their efforts to undermine religious belief by explaining it physiologically. It never occurs to these folks, complains James, to trace to an author's "neurotic constitution" any ideas they find attractive. Why not explain through neurology the triumphs of industry and the arts and science itself? "Let us play fair in this whole matter," he remonstrates; "physiological theory" can do just as well at explaining nonreligious states of mind as religious states of mind, and in neither case would such a theory tell us all we need to know about its object.[17]

Right from the start, then, in that opening chapter, James invokes what he eventually calls his "objective conscience." This is the voice he associates with the demands of science, rightly understood: the uniformitarianism, the fair play, the public knowledge, the intersubjective testing of truth claims against the totality of human experience. In the final paragraph of his concluding chapter, James also invokes what he calls his "subjective conscience," the voice he associates with the demands of his religious heritage, with what attracts him to George Fox, with all that is implied when he speaks finally at the end of the book of himself as a "Christian."[18] Indeed, the last few sentences of "Conclusions," when James's scientific conscience and his religious conscience are brought together, constitute one of his most compact and agonistic expressions of the tension by which so much of his life was defined.

James comes to this climactic moment, among the most moving discursive episodes in the more than forty years of Jamesean prose about this problem, when he is trying to explain what he has just declared to be his "over-belief" that God exists and that as human beings open themselves to God their "deepest destiny is fulfilled." "My objective and my subjective conscience both hold me" to that over-belief, he says. Thus fortified by this dual assertion—the two consciences finally driving him the same way, a consummation so long elusive—James then brings his Gifford Lectures to their final sentence, striking for its candid, if tentative affirmation, in the form of a question, of liberal Protestantism's trust in the response of a benevolent God to the righteous strivings of his creatures: "Who knows whether the faithfulness of individuals here below to their own poor over-beliefs may not actually help God in turn to be more effectively faithful to his own greater tasks?"[19]

But while the Gifford Lectures end with that captivating sentence, *Varieties*, the published book, does not. The religious conscience and the scientific conscience, pasted together in act of assertion, continued to pull James in different directions. So he added the tortured, six-page "Postscript," which displays his uncertainty about the issues on which he had pronounced in his concluding chapter. He expresses concern he had not been clear about his "philosophical position." Then we learn that when James had called himself a Christian at Edinburgh he did not mean "to accept either popular Christianity or scholastic theism." We learn, further, that James is a very special kind of supernaturalist, a "piecemeal" supernaturalist to be distinguished from the sort who assigns the whole world to God's providence. James imagines a patchwork cosmos, with supernatural power here or there, one is not sure just where. At pains to remind his readers that he is not a theologian, yet having raised issues of an indisputably theological character, James quickly exits, saying, "I hope to return to the same questions in another book."[20] That is the way *Varieties* actually ends.

At the end of *Varieties*, then, we see James in a decidedly stuttering mode, having allowed himself to pile up example after example of religious experience while putting off the philosophical harvest. His need for a commodious science and a flexible religion was manifest, and *Varieties* had been, among other things, a search for both. But the search was not over. James managed in *Varieties* to articulate more vividly than ever before his loyalty to modern science's principles of intersubjective testability and professional consensus, and his loyalty to a worldview in which supernatural power of the sort posited by his own cultural tradition was an authentic presence and agent of undetermined scope. Neither loyalty was new to James in 1902, but now he was really out there on both.

How did he get there, and where did he go next?

At the risk of making James's life seem more of an integrated whole than it was, I want to quote a few passages from a letter he wrote to Holmes in 1868, when he was twenty-six years old. This letter was written from Germany, where James was studying the new empirical psychology in the wake of a personally distressing time in Brazil on the Agassiz expedition, and before his celebrated mental collapse of 1870 back in Massachusetts. James is telling Holmes how things are coming together for him in Dresden, how he is adopting "an empiricist view of life."

> I don't know how far it will carry me, or what rocks insoluable by it will block my future path. Already I see an ontological cloud of absolute idealism waiting for me far off on the horizon. . . . I shall continue to apply empirical principles to my experiences as I go and see how much they fit.

Here the enduring rivalry between empiricism and Hegelian metaphysics is emplotted, and the work-it-out-as-you-go style of coping with experience is essayed. Then James expresses his uncertainty about how candidly people like himself and the similarly advanced Holmes should share with the less enlightened populace their understanding that the old faiths have been discredited by Darwin and his kind.

If . . . we must take our sensations as simply given or as preserved
by natural selection for us, and interpret this rich and delicate over-
growth of ideas, moral, artistic, religious and social, as a mere mask,
a tissue spun in happy hours by creative individuals and adopted by
other men in the interests of their sensations. . . . How long can we
indulge the "people" in their theological and other vagaries so long
as such vagaries seem to us more beneficial on the whole than otherwise? How long are we to wear that uncomfortable "air of sup-
pression" which has been complained of [by] Mill?

James continues by pondering if there might be a way to salvage something from the old religion. Perhaps we can advance "happiness among
the multitudes," he suggests to Holmes, if we appropriate from "the old
moralities and theologies" a piece of lumber for "our own purposes."
What might that old lumber look like, once appropriated and reworked?
Perhaps, James continues, we can preach "the doctrine that Man is his
own Providence, and every individual a real God to his race, greater or
less in proportion to his gifts and the way he uses them?" Then James, in-
voking the capacity of modern human beings for solidarity with one another in worldly ventures, speculates that "philanthropy" might take the
place of religion "as an ultimate motive for human action."[21]

Now, James certainly did take a piece of lumber from the old religion,
and he did try to build upon it a more frankly humanistic worldview that
would be capable of inspiring the multitudes. The notion of human beings exercising their own "Providence," individually and collectively, was
a grand leitmotif of James's creative work all the way to the time of his
death. Here in 1868 we do find several of the major components of
James's life project. The old religion has something we probably still
need, but it has to be radically humanized, and integrated somehow into
an empiricist understanding of inquiry and of the objects of inquiry. The
most formidable intellectual obstacle to such a program is absolute idealism. The great empiricist John Stuart Mill is someone whose instructions
are worth following. And we should respect the public and try to speak
honestly to it.

These components of James's life project were visible all through the
1870s, 1880s, and early 1890s, even when he saw himself chiefly as a psychologist. They are most prominently displayed in some of the most

widely quoted and reprinted of James's essays during that period, including "The Sentiment of Rationality," "Reflex Arc and Theism," and "Is Life
Worth Living." These can be seen as warm-ups for "The Will to Believe,"
alongside which James reprinted them in 1897 in the book of that title.
These essays sympathize with the religious believer against those hyper-
scientific thinkers who make what James thought was the serious mistake
of assuming that science had ruled out the taking of God seriously. Yet
the essays, at the same time, reflect on the value of science and condemn
the perpetuation of truly anachronistic religious beliefs in a scientific age.

In these essays James invokes the strategy of separate spheres for keeping alive something of the old faith. In "Sentiment of Rationality," first
published in its complete form in 1882, James draws an important distinction. He refers to "a certain class of truths" in regard to which "faith" is appropriate, and that are not supported by "scientific evidence." His favorite
examples tend toward the power of positive thinking, such as believing on
faith that it is really true that you have the ability to leap across an abyss in
order to avoid death. But such examples are embedded in James's standard screed against W. K. Clifford and the agnostics, and his frequent em-
pathic references to holders of religious faith. James's readers are thus invited to think of their decisions about religious belief as analogous to
deciding whether "to bail out a boat because I am in doubt whether my efforts will keep her afloat." So, some truths are real for us on faith, James
says, and others are real for us because of scientific evidence. He concludes
"The Sentiment of Rationality" by celebrating "faith's sphere," which he
describes as "another realm into which the stifled soul may escape from
pedantic scruples." There are risks to this, but many people will find them
worthwhile. Let people do all they can, urges James, "to mark out distinc-
tively the questions which fall within faith's sphere."[22]

James's language does little to disguise the protective character of the
separate spheres doctrine. But by the time of "The Will to Believe" he had
become more cautious. The salient distinction is not as prominent as it
had been before, because it is now surrounded by distinctions between
hypotheses that are living and dead, forced or avoidable, and momentous
or trivial. "The Will to Believe" also contains a much more extensive and
distracting polemic against Clifford for his absurd claim that one can
never do anything except on the basis of sufficient evidence. That was a
canard, as I have shown elsewhere,[23] but here I will ignore James's blatant

misrepresentations of the conveniently deceased Clifford to move quickly on to the highly developed language of tolerance that most distinguishes "The Will to Believe" from the other essays in the series that em-
ploy the separate spheres strategy.

In that legendary essay, the most widely disseminated and quoted item
ever to flow from James's pen, James rests the case for religious belief
heavily upon a general appeal to the principle of "live and let live." He
calls upon everyone to respect one another's beliefs except when those beliefs have been uncontrovertibly disproved. "We ought . . . delicately and
profoundly to respect one another's mental freedom . . . then and only
then we shall have that spirit" of tolerance that is "empiricism's glory."
Thus James subtly relocates the question of true belief out of the jurisdic-
tion of the laboratory and the seminar and places it instead under the ju-
risdiction of the polite drawing room. This sphere of tolerance applies on
one side of the distinction upon which James's argument most turns: the
distinction between questions that can be decided "on intellectual
grounds" and those that "by nature" cannot. Clifford was right about
how science worked, said James, and certainly about the need to believe
"ethically." But Clifford was just plain wrong about the specific cognitive
terrain in which the scientific conscience was to operate. In "The Will to
Believe" James draws the line between scientifically warranted beliefs and
the rest of our opinions more sharply than the positivist Clifford ever did,
and James pushes that line back selectively until it no longer threatens the
varieties of supernaturalism favored by the most theologically liberal of
Protestant believers.[24]

But no sooner did James provide the separate spheres doctrine with
one of the most successful formulations in that doctrine's long history
than he began to back away from it. In the very preface to *The Will to Believe*, the 1897 book the title essay of which James had written the year before and delivered as lectures to student groups at Yale and Brown uni-
versities, James calls for the verification of "religious hypotheses" along
with "scientific hypotheses" by "experimental tests." The emphasis in this
preface, which asks religious believers to come out of "hiding" and actually celebrates the rough-and-tumble, "survival of the fittest" competition
of religious as well as scientific ideas in the public "market-place," is strikingly different from the protective emphasis found in "The Will to Believe" itself, and in the other essays collected with it.[25] I am not sure why

James began, even in 1897, to pull away from what he had just articulated so vividly. Perhaps its metaphysical character bothered him once he confronted in print what he had said. The notion that certain questions have a nature that prevents them from being decided on the basis of evidence and reasoning is, after all, in some respects very non-Jamesean. It sounds like a metaphysical principle, rather out of keeping with James's empiricist determination to take things as they come. In any event, he took a very different approach to religious belief immediately after the publication of "The Will to Believe."

The following year, 1898, James delivered at Berkeley "Philosophical Conceptions and Practical Results," the lecture that became famous for James's declaring himself a "pragmatist," for bringing the ideas of Charles Peirce out of obscurity, and for beginning the discussion of pragmatism that would animate philosophers for the next fifteen years. James quickly published this lecture in the *Journal of Philosophy* under the title, "The Pragmatic Method."[26] Now, a remarkable feature of this text that is almost never discussed is the fact that it is almost entirely about God. Yet, unlike "The Will to Believe," where God talk is carefully circumscribed, the Berkeley lecture is almost never anthologized or even cited in discussions of science and religion. It is true that James says he is only using the God question as an example of the power of Peirce's principle of pragmatism. And it is true that James does not explicitly defend the claim that God exists. No doubt there are other reasons for this lecture's having found its way into the history of philosophy canon but not into the religious studies canon. But the simple point I want to make is that in it James experiments with an epistemically monolithic context for deciding religious issues.

James does not flag this move. But he makes it. First he applies to the idea of God Peirce's principle that to get a clear idea of something, "we need only consider what effects of a conceivably practical kind the object may involve—what sensations we are to expect from it, and what reactions we must prepare." It is in pursuit of this epistemically universal method that James then analyzes how different are the effects of theism and materialism. But James reinforces the move again at the end of the lecture when he interprets Peirce as having simply sharpened the empiricist tradition of Locke, Hume, and Mill. James concludes with a ringing affirmation of the philosophical tradition of English empiricism,[27] within which the God talk of the lecture is thus quietly embraced. When James wrote *Pragmatism* in 1907 he dedicated it, after all, to the free-thinking empiricist Mill, even while offering that book as a way of widening the search for God.

Before turning to that book, however, I want to note that James invokes something he calls "pragmatism" three times in *Varieties,* which, please recall, James wrote after he gave the Berkeley lecture but before he wrote *Pragmatism.* In the first use of the word "pragmatism" in *Varieties,* James uses it against the metaphysicians who prattle on about various attributes of God; what difference could it possibly make, he asks as a self-styled pragmatist, if God has the attribute of "simplicity" or "necessariness"? Here, James is simply tracking passages from his 1898 lecture, and providing a more cogent and compelling summary of Peirce than he had managed to do previously. A few pages later, he alludes to the same pragmatic denial that metaphysical argumentation about God's attributes matters one whit. James's third and most interesting reference is on the final page of his concluding chapter, where he describes as a "thoroughly 'pragmatic' view of religion" the view that higher powers actually affect the course of the world, and are not simply in charge of it in some general, detached way. This view, he says, has generally been accepted by "common men," who have believed in "miracles" and have "built a heaven out beyond the grave."[28] Here James associates the name of pragmatism with some very strong claims about divine agency, and it is presumably just these passages that he was most worried about when he appended his postscript, cautioning that he is not a Christian in the common man's sense after all, nor a theist in the scholastic's sense.

In that postscript James does something else that marks the transitional character of *Varieties.* He renounces for the first time, as Wayne Proudfoot has observed in a recent article in the *Harvard Theological Review,* the notion that God's guarantee of a permanent moral order is central to theism.[29] James had still asserted this in his Berkeley lecture, and he repeated it again in the conclusion to *Varieties.* Yet in the postscript James structures theism as accommodating the taking of a risk rather than the acceptance of a guarantee. "A final philosophy of religion," he speculates, will have to accept a "pluralistic" hypothesis according to which only part of the world will be saved and part will be lost, and the outcome will depend to a degree on what human beings do.[30] And here at last we are at the cusp of what James delivered a few years later in *Pragmatism*.

In that book, where he speaks repeatedly of the world's salvation, as he does in his related correspondence, James invites religious believers to risk their beliefs in inquiry, to renounce the safe harbors of the metaphysicians and to confront the materialists on their own ground, which was experience in the world.[31] Here the episteme is monolithic, the fate of religion feels less secure, but the chances of vindication ostensibly much greater than in the cloistered cognitive world of the metaphysicians and other world-eschewing believers. This is, James implies but never says explicitly, because outside is where you find the field of struggle on which the future of culture will be decided. That field is the field of intersubjective empirical inquiry. But to see how James carries this off in *Pragmatism*, we need to focus on three sequential elements of that text: its opening frame, what it declares the doctrine of "pragmatism" to be, and the final chapter, entitled "Pragmatism and Religion," which unfortunately is one of the least carefully studied of all the things James wrote under the sign of pragmatism.

James's opening leaves not the slightest doubt that he wrote *Pragmatism* for people worried about the fate of religion in the face of the advance of science. The book begins by confronting the concerned soul with an obviously unacceptable choice between "tough-minded" empiricist-skeptics and "tender-minded" religious idealists. James then offers a solution: he lays out pragmatism as a middle way, suitable for those too tender to give up on God but too tough to give up on science.[32]

But when James tells us "What Pragmatism Means"—the second element in the text to which I call attention—he offers what turns out to be a natural history of belief. He describes how human beings, as a behavioral fact, form their ideas and change them in the course of experience, both individually and collectively. Especially, he points to how scientific ideas change, how ideas we take to be true in one generation are so often replaced by other ideas later. We hold to our old ideas as much as we can, but new experience puts them under strain, so we graft some new idea "upon the ancient stock" while dropping some of the old opinions. The body of truth, then, "grows much as a tree grows by the activity of a new layer of cambium."[33] Although this natural history of belief echoed points James had made here and there in his previous writings, never before had he developed so sustained an account of the dependence of scientific truth upon the cognitive activities of historically situated human communities. When he used to talk about the role of preconceptions in the creation of knowledge, he would usually do so with reference to an individual mind, and while separating out from this process the religious beliefs that science—contrary to the pretensions of freethinkers like Clifford—could not touch. Now, in 1907, he nested the problem of religious belief firmly in the same matrix of inquiry with the problem of scientific belief, which is precisely where Peirce had located it way back in 1877 in "Fixation of Belief."[34]

The contrast between Roycean metaphysical idealism and pragmatism dominates the concluding chapter, "Pragmatism and Religion." There, James compares the idealists to the prodigal son, who doesn't really risk anything because he knows he can count on his father to make everything all right in the end. "We want a universe," he mocks the absolutists, "where we can just give up, fall on our father's neck, and be absorbed into the absolute life as a drop of water melts into the river or sea." This is not a realistic view of our human situation, says James. Life as actually lived, as available to an empiricist, suggests that we reside in an uncertain universe with real conflicts and real victories and real defeats. In such a world we cannot take anything for granted, including the salvation of those who are justified by faith. James is saying to members of his own religious tribe that in order to vindicate even the most rudimentary aspects of the old faith, they have got to come to grips with the radical contingency of the human process by which culture is created, reproduced, and critically revised. Once you clue into this, he implies, then you have to try to get your ideas accepted within this process, not by ignoring it. James calls his tribe to "a social scheme of co-operative work," a project that requires its participants to "trust" each other as they work together.[35] There is no guarantee that your culture will survive without your own hard work, no guarantee that the sensibilities you hold dear will continue to find social support in the decades and centuries to come; but at least you can try to make it so. Don't let Royce tell you, James implicitly scolds, that he has proved logically that we are all embraced within the Absolute.

"Must *all* be saved?" James begins a series of increasingly jagged rhetorical questions designed to undermine the ultimate cheerfulness and complacency of the idealists.

Is *no* price to be paid for the work of salvation? Is the last word sweet? Is all "yes, yes" in the universe? Doesn't the fact of "no" stand at the very core of life? Doesn't the very "seriousness" that we attribute to life mean that ineluctable noes and losses form a part of it, that . . . at the bottom of the cup something "permanently drastic and bitter always remains"?[36]

In these final pages of *Pragmatism*, James simultaneously attacks the idealists and reassures his audience that he has not become an atheist. "I have written a book on men's religious experience," James says proudly of *Varieties*, "which on whole has been regarded as making for the reality of God." And in these final pages James reverts again and again to the problem of the world's salvation, and to the role that human beings might play in it by working in harmony with God, whom James describes as "but one helper" amid "all the shapers of the great world's fate." If we do our part right, there is at least a possibility that "when the cup" of life is "finally poured off," what we drink will be "sweet enough" even if "the dregs are left behind forever."[37] How do we humans do our part to maximize our chances of gaining this sweetness?

Well, one thing we can do is to "bring the evidence in," James says, to support our "over-beliefs," including the over-belief that God exists and is responsive to our strivings. James ends *Pragmatism* with an evangelical call to religious believers to come out of idealist shelters and set sail on the risky seas of experience, bringing in evidence of the sort that might actually stand up in the structure of plausibility that counted in the modern, North Atlantic West. The risk, of course, was that the religious hypothesis might not stand up: perhaps experience might not confirm what one hoped it would. We need to take the "hypothesis of God," James says, inserting religion directly into the discourse of empirical inquiry, and "build it out," so that the evidence it generates can "combine satisfactorily with all the other working truths" we possess.[38] James thus places the God question directly in the natural history of belief that he has presented as the core of pragmatism. This is a long way from "The Will to Believe." The distinction between questions that can be resolved by evidence and those that cannot has—quietly!—all but disappeared.

If there is any doubt about what is going on in these last few intense pages of *Pragmatism*, which rival the conclusions to *Varieties* for their combination of anxiety and conviction, James conflates his own call to believers to throw themselves into empirical inquiry with the call of a shipwrecked sailor who died in a storm yet through his epitaph bids others "to set sail," because "many a gallant bark, when we were lost, Weathered the gale." Moreover, as soon as James quotes the epitaph, he links this bold sailing into the storm with the willingness of the old Puritans to accept an uncertain world and take chances in the hope that their risk-taking acts would be instruments for God's purposes. "Are you willing," he asks his contemporary American Protestants in the voice of the old Puritans—calling upon his friends to risk their beliefs in inquiry on the hope that they will be more commandingly vindicated—"to be damned for God's glory?"[39]

James follows this question with an uncharacteristically perfectionist passage about the future of the globe, suggesting the possibility of saving the world by actually eliminating evil, and he does so while contrasting his mode of worldly struggle with Royce's mode of "aufgehoben":

> [My] way of escape from evil . . . is not by getting it "aufgehoben,"
> or preserved in the whole as an element essential but "overcome."
> *It is by dropping* [evil] *out altogether, throwing it overboard and getting beyond it, helping to make a universe that shall forget* [evil's] *very place and name.*[40]

Now, the extremity of this last passage, nearly all of which James renders in italics, is remarkable enough. And here is another of James's maritime figures of speech, with the hardy protagonists of his cosmic narrative in a boat struggling to throw evil "overboard." But the passage that follows this anomalous effusion of religious perfectionism, revealing a yearning for spiritual consummation that James normally kept in the shadows, is even more interesting for anyone trying to assess what James meant by "pragmatism" and how his development of it relates to the preoccupations of *Varieties*. Whoever is "willing to live on a scheme of uncertified possibilities which he trusts; willing to pay with his own person, if need be for the realization of the ideals which he frames"—and this is a secular translation of whoever is willing to be "damned for God's glory"—is a "genuine pragmatist."[41] This sense of pragmatism has much in common with that displayed on the last page of *Varieties*, where, as I noted earlier, "pragmatism" is associated with the doctrine that the world is the site of a struggle of uncertain outcome, in which there is at least a chance that supernatural agencies and virtuous human strivings might work together for good.

Reading the *Pragmatism* of 1907, then, helps us see what James was working toward when he wrote *Varieties* in 1902. And if we have *Varieties* in mind when we read *Pragmatism*, we are better able to grasp the depth and character of the religious concerns that produced the often enigmatic formulations James offered under the sign of "pragmatism." Shortly after 1897 James seems to have come to the conclusion that the strategy of keeping the essence of religion safely protected from the structures of plausibility being inculcated in modern societies by science was a dead end. His sponsorship of the epistemically monolithic Peirce and his adoption of what was, for James, a new label, "pragmatism," mark the start of his own risky voyage, the first substantial vessel for which was *Varieties*. He later built and sailed on other ships, most of which we continue to study, as we study *Varieties*, without attending to the course James himself had charted for them. We are not obliged to accept his priorities in order to learn from what he wrote, but we are less likely to project our own ideas onto his if we know what he was trying to do and recognize the lights and shadows that affected his vision.

Did James "turn the lights down low so as to give miracle a chance"? No doubt he did, but at the same time he replaced the fierce concept of "miracle" with the bland-sounding "the religious hypothesis." James rendered religion so general that it had a much better chance of being accepted in the modern structure of plausibility than did any particular religious doctrine. He worked from both ends simultaneously, making science more commodious and religion less confined by anything that might conflict with any specific finding of science.

Two years after James was born, a close friend of his parents wrote:

> Truth forever on the scaffold,
> Wrong forever on the throne. . . .

James Russell Lowell, in "The Present Crisis," continued,[42]

> Yet that scaffold sways the future, and
> Behind the dim unknown
> Standeth God within the shadow
> Keeping watch above his own.

I believe that William James always hoped, in part of his soul, that God would come out of the New England shadow invoked by Lowell, that Yahweh would speak to him from the whirlwind, show him the burning bush, let him see Ezekiel's wheel in the middle of the sky. But nothing like that ever happened. It was James's destiny rather to become his generation's most creative and conspicuous case simultaneously of the radical liberalization of Protestantism and of the radical historicization of scientific inquiry. In achieving this place in a history that we can recognize a century after the fact, I suppose James himself may have been damned, and perhaps even for God's glory, but that uncertainty in James studies is one that I leave well enough alone.

NOTES

For helpful comments on a draft of this paper, I wish to thank Wayne Proudfoot, Richard Rorty, Mark Schwehn, and Ann Taves.

1. Oliver Wendell Holmes Jr., to Frederick Pollock, September 1, 1910, in *Holmes-Pollock Letters, The Correspondence of Mr. Justice Holmes and Sir Frederick Pollock, 1874–1932,* 2 vols., ed. Mark DeWolfe Howe (Cambridge: Harvard University Press, 1941), I:67.

2. William James, *The Varieties of Religious Experience* (Cambridge: Harvard University Press, 1985), 359–360.

3. Richard R. Niebuhr, "William James on Religious Experience," in *The Cambridge Companion to William James,* ed. Ruth Anna Putnam (Cambridge and New York: Cambridge University Press, 1997), 225.

4. James, *Varieties,* 15–16. For an example of the use in James's milieu of this famous phrase of Huxley's, see David Starr Jordan, "Comrades in Zeal," *Popular Science Monthly* 64 (1904): 304.

5. John E. Smith, "Introduction" to James, *Varieties,* xxxvi.

6. James, *Varieties,* 217–218.

7. Ibid. 229.

8. Ibid. 241–249.

9. Ibid. 272–283, 265.

10. Ibid. 266, 277, 295, 297.

11. Ibid. 266.

12. For Gordon, see William Hutchison, *The Modernist Impulse in American Protestantism* (Cambridge: Harvard University Press, 1976), 234–244. It should be acknowledged that James's sympathies for idiosyncratic and extreme religious persuasions set him somewhat apart from the high decorum style of the liberal Protestant establishment.

13. James, *Varieties,* 342, 359.

14. Ibid. 359.

15. Ibid. 358.

16. Ibid. 402, 411.

17. Ibid. 20–22.

18. Ibid. 406, 408.

19. Ibid. 408.

20. Ibid. 409–414.

21. William James to Oliver Wendell Holmes Jr., May 18, 1868, in Ralph Barton Perry, *The Thought and Character of William James*, 2 vols. (Boston: Little, Brown, 1935), I:516–517.

22. William James, *The Will to Believe* (Cambridge: Harvard University Press, 1979), 80, 88–89.

23. David A. Hollinger, "James, Clifford, and the Scientific Conscience," in *Companion*, ed. Putnam, 69–83.

24. James, *The Will to Believe*, 20, 33.

25. Ibid. 8–9.

26. The text of "The Pragmatic Method" is reprinted in William James, *Essays in Philosophy* (Cambridge: Harvard University Press, 1978), 123–139.

27. Ibid. 124.

28. James, *Varieties*, 351, 361, 408.

29. Wayne Proudfoot, "William James on an Unseen Order," *Harvard Theological Review* 93, 1 (2000): 51–66.

30. James, *Varieties*, 414.

31. The analysis of *Pragmatism* developed here expands upon points made in David A. Hollinger, *In the American Province: Studies in the History and Historiography of Ideas* (Bloomington: Indiana University Press, 1985), 4–22.

32. William James, *Pragmatism* (Cambridge: Harvard University Press, 1978), 13.

33. Ibid. 34–36.

34. Charles Peirce, "The Fixation of Belief," *Popular Science Monthly* 12 (1877): 1–15.

35. James, *Pragmatism*, 139–140.

36. Ibid. 141.

37. Ibid. 142–143.

38. Ibid. 143–144.

39. Ibid. 142.

40. Ibid.

41. Ibid.

42. James Russell Lowell, "The Present Crisis," in *The Complete Poetical Works of James Russell Lowell*, ed. Horace E. Scudder (Boston: Houghton Mifflin, 1896), 67.

2

✧

Pragmatism and "an Unseen Order" in *Varieties*

WAYNE PROUDFOOT

Religious thinkers considering the relation between science and religion often stress the autonomy of the latter. Religion is not in the business of explaining the world; it provides an interpretation of a different sort: meaning, not causal explanation. If complete, this separation would preclude any conflict between the two realms. Claims in one would have nothing to do with those in the other. But it is not easy to keep them apart. The meanings that inform people's lives can't be sharply distinguished from the ways in which they make sense of what is happening to them in light of their best explanations of themselves and their world.

James addresses this issue in *Varieties*. He distinguishes at the outset between explaining religious experience on one hand and evaluating it or judging its significance on the other, and works throughout the book to keep these tasks separate. But his particular conception of religion and his worry about what he takes to be the implications of a scientific naturalism make that separation very difficult to sustain. I will first describe what

James means by religion and what kind of inquiry he takes himself to be pursuing in *Varieties*. Then I will argue that the question of the adequacy of natural explanations of religious experience looms large for him, even though he explicitly says that he will set it aside. Finally, I will consider James's evaluation of the benefits and drawbacks of particular types of religious experience, and suggest how his account might be modified to preserve his evaluation and to overcome his worries about naturalism.

I

Were he asked to give a general characterization of religion, James says in *Varieties*, he would describe it as "the belief that there is an unseen order, and that our supreme good lies in harmoniously adjusting ourselves thereto. This belief and this adjustment are the religious attitude in the soul."[1] This issue of an unseen order—of how to understand it, and of the different ways religious people take themselves to stand in relation to it—is the chief topic of the book. It is a topic that had long preoccupied him, and that pervades all his writings on religion. In a recent lecture at Berkeley, James had identified the idea of God with a guarantee of an ideal order, and added, "this need of an eternal moral order is one of the deepest needs of our breast."[2] Twenty years earlier, he had written that the radical question of life is whether this be at bottom a moral or an unmoral universe, whether it is congruous with our spontaneous powers.[3] The sense of "moral" here is not restricted to ethics, but is the sense in which the moral sciences, comprising what we now call humanities and the social sciences, were contrasted in the nineteenth century with the natural sciences. To ask whether the universe is moral or unmoral is to ask whether it is shaped to human thought and action. The alternative, for James, is what he views as a block universe of blind causation. His talk in *Varieties* of an unseen order is mean to capture this broader sense of "moral."

During the 1880s James and Friedrich Nietzsche each published a series of essays describing religion as belief in an unseen moral order.[4] Nietzsche's attitude toward that belief was very different from James's. Like James, he viewed the need for a moral order as a deep one. Unlike James, he believed that need should be overcome and rooted out so that people might understand themselves and the world more clearly. The idea of divine providence, as represented in the Bible and in subsequent theologies of history, with its assumption of a will of God that gives meaning to history, is an idea of a moral world order.[5] But, Nietzsche says, it is a deception. This world is anything but divine, he writes in *The Gay Science*; "we have interpreted it far too long in a false and mendacious way, in accordance with the wishes of our reverence, which is to say, according to our *needs*."[6]

Talk of an eternal moral order in both James and Nietzsche echoes Matthew Arnold's 1873 depiction of the biblical idea of God as "an eternal power, not ourselves, that makes for righteousness."[7] "Eternal," in Arnold's phrase as in James's, is a way of emphasizing that this order is not man-made; it is "not ourselves." "I simply refuse," James wrote to a friend, "to accept the notion of there being *no* purpose in the objective world."[8] The issue posed by James's view of religion is whether or not there is any moral order in the universe, any unseen order with which people can bring themselves into harmony, that is not something that humans have put there. His language—"radical question," "deepest need," "simply refuse to accept"—shows that he thought that a lot is at stake in how this question is resolved.

In a striking image early in *Varieties,* James offers a picture of a world with no such order. "For naturalism," he writes, "fed on recent cosmological speculations, mankind is in a position similar to that of a set of people living on a frozen lake, surrounded by cliffs over which there is no escape, yet knowing that little by little the ice is melting, and the inevitable day drawing near when the last film of it will disappear, and to be drowned ignominiously will be the human creature's portion. The merrier the skating, the warmer and more sparkling the sun by day, and the ruddier the bonfires at night, the more poignant the sadness with which one must take in the meaning of the total situation."[9]

In articles written over two decades James reflects on how to adjudicate the dispute between theism and the position he variously identifies as atheism, materialism, and naturalism. In the preface to *The Will to Believe*, written while he was negotiating to give the lectures that became *Varieties*, James says that all beliefs are fallible, and the only way religious hypotheses can be tested is by experiments in living, by people actively living their faiths and trying to discover which works best. This, he says, is the method employed in scientific inquiry. "Works best" here includes, importantly, considerations of how these beliefs accord with a person's best explanations of herself and the world. "Religious history proves," he says, "that one hypothesis after another has worked ill, has crumbled with a widening knowledge of the world, and has lapsed from the minds of men."[10]

A year later in the Berkeley lecture, James again picks up this project. The lecture is well known for the first public use of the term "pragmatism," but James also described it as a rehearsal for *Varieties*.[11] On this occasion he introduces Charles Peirce's pragmatic method for making ideas clear. To clarify a thought, Peirce said, we must consider the practical effects the object of the thought would have, and how it might affect our conduct. Peirce has scientific experimentation in mind. When we say that a diamond is hard, for instance, we mean that our attempts to scratch it with most materials will fail. James broadens Peirce's criterion to include what is passively experienced as well as what effects we might expect as a consequence of our actions. In this way he detaches it from scientific inquiry, while still emphasizing the need to articulate the difference a belief would make for a person's life.

Attempting to clarify the idea of "God," James says that it means a guarantee of an ideal order that shall be permanently preserved.[12] It is a license for hope. Even if the world were to burn up or freeze, God would bring his ideals to fruition. The question of God's existence is trivial, he says, viewed as an abstract theological question, but it is significant if we test it by its results for actual life. Religious doctrine is parasitic on specific experiences directly connected to feeling and conduct,such as voices and visions, responses to prayer, changes of heart, deliverances from fear, assurances of support, and redirection of internal attitudes. *Varieties* is a survey of these and other forms of religious experience in order to assess their bearing on the question of an ideal order and its consequences for life.

II

James devotes much of the book to showing that people actively living by their faiths experience real effects, and that in religious practice real work is done. He cites reports of healing, lifting of depression, overcoming addictions, radical reordering of priorities, and claims for the efficacy of prayer. He also considers mystical experience. *Varieties* has too often been read with an almost exclusive focus on the chapter on mysticism. Read this way, it is a contribution to the epistemology of religious experience conceived as analogous to ordinary sense perception. But this is to truncate the book. James's conclusions about the epistemic value of mystical experience are much more circumspect than is often recognized. Among the experiences people report are what seem to some to be moments of insight into a wider world of meaning not available in ordinary experience. Anything that comes from such a moment, he says, is only a hypothesis. It must be sifted and tested just as we test what comes from the outer world by way of our senses.

Religion differs from morality, James thinks, by the fact that it provides a new zest, an influx of energy. Morality consists of obligations a person knows she must fulfill, or goods toward which she must strive. She or the larger community must work to bring those goods about, or at least to make progress toward them. Morality depends solely on human effort, what James refers to as an athletic attitude. When that attitude breaks down and a person becomes "all sicklied o'er with the sense of irremediable impotence," she may experience what seems like help from outside. Tension yields to calm, fear is expunged, and new energy is released. "Religious feeling," he writes, "is an absolute addition to the Subject's range of life. It gives him a new sphere of power. . . . If religion is to mean anything definite for us, it seems to me that we ought to take it as meaning this added dimension of emotion . . . in regions where morality strictly so called can at best but bow its head and acquiesce."[13] The strenuous life, the willingness to take risks and to persevere in the face of opposition, is to be found, James says, in religion if it is to be found anywhere.

The principal example James offers of real change is conversion. Religious revivals were a central feature of popular Protestant piety in the nineteenth century, and reports of dramatic conversion widespread. He quotes a number at length. A Connecticut man privately publishes an account of his life from the age of five to twenty-four, culminating in the night on which he felt the presence of the Holy Spirit. Alphonse Ratisbonne, a freethinking French Jew, steps into a church in Rome, and has what he takes to be a miraculous vision of the Virgin. "Were we writing a story of the mind from the purely natural-history point of view," James says, "with no religious interest whatever, we should still have to write down man's liability to sudden and complete conversion as one of his most curious peculiarities."[14]

III

What bearing does any of this have on the issue James identified at Berkeley as the pragmatic difference between theism and materialism—the existence of a moral order that is eternal, that is not something that men and women themselves have put there? The religious life may bring with it the effects he surveys. But why should we think that these effects can't be explained in purely naturalistic terms, the terms of history and the social sciences?

A number of the conversion narratives are drawn from material collected by his student Edwin Starbuck, who thought conversion a normal adolescent phenomenon that may be accelerated and intensified in evangelical settings. James himself employs observations and theories from his *The Principles of Psychology*,[15] where he argues that willing is a matter of fixing attention and holding it on a particular idea or end. When attention is focused on a goal, neurological and physiological processes are called into play along pathways well worn by habit, and action follows. In *Varieties* he describes conversion as an alteration of the vital or hot places in a person's field of consciousness, bringing with it a change in her habitual center of personal energy. Emotional and behavioral change results from this altered focus of attention that redirects energy into new pathways. His theory of will as selective attention enables James to assume that a change in the field of consciousness, or alteration of attention, will lead to action and practical consequences. In a different example, he compares the sense of insight in conversion with the experience of suddenly remembering a name after active searching and repeated frustration. In some cases, when one gives up, relaxes, and turns her attention to something else the name comes to mind, seemingly from nowhere.

How, then, do the emotional and behavioral changes James catalogues throughout the book have any bearing on the question of the existence of some unseen order that is "not ourselves"? Does it make any difference, any religious difference, whether these effects can be exhaustively explained in naturalistic terms? His answer, at least in the dominant line of his narrative, is clear: it doesn't matter at all.

James distinguishes sharply in the opening pages of *Varieties* between an explanation of an emotion, event, or mental state and a judgment concerning its spiritual value or significance.[16] These issues are orthogonal, and the judgments must be made independently of one another. Recent biblical scholarship, he says, is a case in point. Research into the origins of the biblical text and the historicity of events reported in it cannot undermine its spiritual value. That is a separate matter requiring a different kind of judgment. It is invulnerable to the results of science or history. Similarly, a neurological explanation of a religious experience tells us nothing about its religious value. The only way to identify genuine religious affections is by their consequences, not their origins; by their fruits, not their roots. He cites Jonathan Edwards to this effect, and says that this is how such judgments are always made, despite the explicit reasons given.[17]

James's clearest statement that a naturalistic explanation of a religious experience would have no bearing on a judgment of its religious significance comes in his discussion of conversion. He speculates that a conversion experience might be explained by incursions from the subconscious into the conscious mind, and that the difference between gradual and instantaneous converts might reflect a difference in susceptibility to work that goes on outside the margins of primary consciousness. "I don't see why the Methodists need object to such a view . . . ," he writes. "You may remember that I argued against the notion that the worth of a thing can be decided by its origin. . . . If the *fruits for life* of the state of conversion are good, we ought to idealize it and venerate it, even though it be a piece of natural psychology; if not, we ought to make short work with it, no matter what supernatural being may have infused it."[18]

IV

That's the dominant line of the narrative. But there is another line as well, one that surfaces first in the chapters on conversion and later in the final pages of the book. I quoted at the outset James's metaphor for a world in which naturalistic explanations are sufficient, a community imprisoned on a frozen lake with melting ice and no escape. Much of the intellectual energy of the book is focused at points at which he addresses the issue of naturalism. His concern to refute or dislodge naturalistic explanations shows how salient the issue is for him.

After a general descriptive account of conversion, James says that psychology and religion are in perfect harmony up to this point, both acknowledging that there are forces seemingly outside the conscious individual that bring redemption. Nevertheless, psychology implies that these forces do not transcend the individual's personality, and in this it diverges from theology.[19] James focuses on psychology, but the issue would be the same if we were to explain these forces by reference to social structures or practices or any other historical products. The question is whether naturalistic explanations are sufficient, or some other force must be invoked.

What do we think? James asks. Is instantaneous conversion a miracle or a natural process? Is it divine in its fruits, but not in its causes?[20] It seems to consist of incursions into the field of consciousness from subliminal or subconscious states. What does that imply? In *Fits, Trances, and Visions* Ann Taves gives an excellent account of the different conceptions of the subconscious offered by Pierre Janet and James's friend, the British psychical researcher Frederick Myers.[21] Janet viewed any manifestation of a secondary self as pathological, while Myers held that subliminal consciousness is a normal effect of the naturally "multiplex" character of mind. The relevance of this difference between normal and pathological lies in what kind of explanation is appropriate. If, with Janet, all manifestations of a secondary self are pathological, or symptoms of hysteria, then the contents of the subconscious can be explained in terms of some physical injury or other trauma in a person's history that might have affected the functioning of her mind. If evidence of these secondary selves can be found in normal, healthy patients, then incursions from the subconscious are not subject to specific explanations of this sort, and their origin remains unaccounted for.

James writes in *Varieties* that "the most important step forward that has occurred in psychology since I have been a student of that science is the discovery . . . of a set of memories, thoughts, and feelings which are extra-marginal and outside of the primary consciousness altogether, but yet must be classed as conscious facts of some sort, able to reveal their presence by unmistakable signs."[22] He cites studies by Janet, Alfred Binet, Josef Breuer, Freud, and others of unconscious memories and their irruption into primary fields of consciousness. In an important footnote he says that psychologists agree that the subconscious is a place "for the accumulation of vestiges of sensible experience," and that the current scientific view is to regard invasive alterations of consciousness as results of the tension of subliminal memories. But, he writes, there are occasional bursts into consciousness that might not be so easily explained in these terms. He cites four cases, including those of Alphonse Ratisbonne and St. Paul. "The result, then," he says, "would have to be ascribed either to a merely physiological nerve storm, a 'discharging lesion' like that of epilepsy; or, in case it were useful and rational . . . to some more mystical or theological hypothesis."[23] James then adds: "I make this remark in order that the reader may realize that the subject is really complex. But I shall keep myself as far as possible at present to the more 'scientific' view; and only as the plot thickens in subsequent lectures shall I consider the question of its absolute sufficiency as an explanation of all the facts. That sub-conscious incubation explains a great number of them, there can be no doubt."[24]

I go into this in some detail because it shows James at work trying to address the question of whether or not religious experience can be explained (explained with "absolute sufficiency") in naturalistic terms. A person who undergoes conversion takes herself to have been acted upon by something outside. A recurrent theme in James's discussion of the effects of conversion and of a robust religious life is a newfound zest, a release of energy, and a reorientation of the self. Here, in this footnote, he considers various explanations for these effects and at the same time defers the question, promising to consider it in "subsequent lectures."

James doesn't see how a naturalistic explanation could account for both force and meaning, both the added zest and energy a convert experiences and the reorientation of consciousness, or direction. He sees how subconscious memories can carry meaning, but doubts that mere association of memories could build up enough tension to burst into consciousness with the kind of force felt by the convert. The alternative explanation in the literature for incursions from the subconscious was physiological, nerves or a disorder like epilepsy, which could explain the force but would not carry any meaning, and therefore could not account for the reorientation.[25] In this footnote James says that if memory associations are insufficient to explain the phenomena, the alternatives are either a physiological hypothesis or a theological one.

James had written a lengthy review of Janet's two-volume study of the mental states of hysterics, followed by a brief notice of the paper by Breuer and Freud in which they describe hysteria as a "disease of memory."[26] The memories released in Breuer's patient by hypnosis and by his sympathy and attention were not static. The authors argued that her associations and symptoms, including partial paralysis, were precipitates of experiences of arousal that had had to be suppressed. When the memories were revived, pent-up emotion was released, and the symptoms disappeared. Freud later argued that such symptoms result from the dynamic relation between a wish and the force required to suppress it. This explanation may or not be right, but it is of the right sort. It accounts for both force and meaning by reference to the patient's history. It shows that the association of memories might not be impotent, as James thought, but might carry the power as well as the meaning content of suppressed wishes.

Another point at which James engages the issue of naturalism is in his discussion of prayer, which he describes very broadly as a consciousness individuals have of intercourse with higher powers with which they feel themselves to be related. If nothing is really transacted in this relation, if no work is done, he says, "then prayer, taken in this wider meaning . . . is of course a feeling of what is illusory, and religion must on the whole be classed, not simply as containing elements of delusion, . . . but as being rooted in delusion altogether, just as materialists and atheists have always said it was."[27]

This is a strong statement. Religion is a delusion and atheists are right if prayer is not a real transaction. If an individual thinks she is related to something outside herself, and the relation is only with another part of her own mind or a product of her mind, it is illusory. What if it is the product not of her mind alone but of history, that is, of other human minds as well? What is the higher power, without which religion is rooted in delusion? James returns to this issue.

Common to all the experiences he has studied, James says, is an individual's consciousness that the higher part of himself is continuous with something "more" of the same quality that is operative in the universe outside of him and with which he can effectively connect.[28] Both "higher part of himself" and "operative in the universe outside of him" are ambiguous. "Higher part" could mean mindlike rather than material, or morally good rather than bad. James means both, but the emphasis here is on the contrast with materialism. The individual feels that this "more" is operative in the universe outside of him, but is it? And, if so, is it the product of the thoughts and actions of men and women?

It is at least the unconscious, James says, and it may well be more than that. Religious thinkers agree that it is more, and this, he thinks, satisfies pragmatism's requirement of a real hypothesis that makes a real difference. Not a hypothesis that can be directly tested, but a claim that one can understand. He strongly criticizes philosophers of religion who say that religion is only an interpretation. It is not, he says, the world of the materialists under a different description. Religion doesn't just illumine facts already given; it posits new facts as well. To settle for anything less is to surrender too easily to naturalism.

We've come a long way from James's claim in the dominant line of his narrative that explanation should have no bearing on the religious significance of an experience. At crucial points he engages the issue, arguing that naturalistic explanations are not sufficient, and that if they were religion would be delusion and we would be left with a world without hope.

V

I have concentrated on James's ambivalence about explanation. I want now to turn briefly to his assessment of the extent to which religious thought and practice contribute to human well-being.

His evaluation of specific religious practices betrays an almost comical Protestant bias.[29] He has no use for ritual. Though he respects the virtues of charity, poverty, and asceticism, he summarily dismisses the forms these take in biographies of Roman Catholic saints. He thinks Louis Gonzaga's extreme ascetic practices reveal an intellect no larger than a pin's head.[30] He admires St. Teresa's intellect, but regrets that so much vitality should have been devoted to such paltry ideals.[31] James makes no attempt to grasp the point of these practices in their particular historical and social contexts; each is evaluated as if it were a proposal for turn-of-the-century Edinburgh or Cambridge. In order to understand these practices and the ways in which they benefit or are detrimental to the individuals who engage in them and to others, one would have to provide a kind of thick description in which he has no interest. But he is right to hold that normative judgments about religious practices are perfectly appropriate in the study of religion, and that they ought to be made explicit and available for discussion and revision.

James's more significant evaluative thesis is set forth in a quiet polemic that is easy to miss because it takes the form of a simple descriptive typology, distinguishing religious optimism from religious pessimism. His terms for these two types are "healthy-mindedness" and "the sick soul." He judges the optimistic type to be superficial and naïve in light of the extent of suffering and evil in the world. James had compared these two religious attitudes twenty years earlier in an introduction to his father's unpublished writings.[32] The chapter in *Varieties* on the sick soul concludes with a disguised account of his own crippling experience of panic fear.[33] This was an issue that engaged him personally as well as professionally.

The popular religious landscape of late nineteenth-century Protestant New England seemed to support James's description of two types of religious attitudes. Revivalism, with its emphasis on acknowledgment of sin and hope for redemption, provided the paradigm for the sick soul. Healthy-mindedness was more diffuse. It included liberal Protestants, the transcendentalist legacy of Ralph Waldo Emerson, and various groups and techniques James referred to as "Mind-cure," including those of Christian Science. They each rejected or liberally reinterpreted the doctrine of sin. Sin, evil, and for some practitioners even illness are illusory. According to this view, everything that is is good. Anxiety, pain, and conflict are transient and can be overcome by adopting the proper attitude. These two types are prominently featured in the religion sections of bookstores today as New Age spirituality and evangelical Christianity. Some books on those shelves today are also cited by James, like Ralph Waldo Trine's *In Tune with the Infinite* and John Bunyan's *Grace Abounding to the Chief of Sinners*.

We know that the world contains large amounts of pain, suffering, and tragedy, James writes, and that it would be better off without them. Any philosophy that fails to acknowledge this doesn't deserve serious consideration. He is particularly critical of the view that pain and tragedy are good because they serve to develop character, an idea he finds in "the last runnings of the romantic school" in French literature.[34] This kind of rationalization, he thinks, opens the way to fanaticism and fatalism. Religious optimism can sustain itself only by massive denial. The revivalist emphasis on sin and the need for transformation captures an important part of experience that is omitted by liberal Protestants, mental scientists, and spiritualists.

James increasingly came to defend a metaphysical pluralism, motivated by the recognition that the world contains forces for both good and evil, as well as by the conviction that knowledge is always partial, piecemeal, and incomplete. Any attempt to bring everything under some unified divine purpose or absolute conception would falsify experience. Polytheism represents this pluralistic view better than monotheism. In the Berkeley lecture James had said that the concept of God means a guarantee of an eternal ideal order. By the time of writing the postscript to *Varieties,* he relinquishes the idea of a guarantee. Religion, he says, requires only the chance that our ideals may be brought to fruition.[35] In the last of his lectures on pragmatism James develops this theme further. The genuine pragmatist requires no guarantee: "He is willing to live on a scheme of uncertified possibilities which he trusts."[36]

VI

The chief obstacle to an appreciation of *Varieties* today, a century after its publication, is likely to be James's lack of attention to historical context. He juxtaposes material from biographies of Counter-Reformation saints with quotations from Tolstoy, Ramakrishna, and contemporary proponents of mind-cure. In fact, James quotes his sources at greater length than is common today among philosophers writing on religious experience, and he pays closer attention to their language. He lifts them out of their contexts because he wants to construct a composite portrait of types of religious experience that he takes to be the same across different historical and cultural settings. James was more aware than most of his contemporaries that the world is shaped by the thoughts and actions of men and women. But he holds open the possibility that the object of religious belief and practice, the unseen order or "more" that is continuous with the higher part of the self, and with which a person can get in touch, is not a product of those thoughts and actions.[37]

James calls for philosophy of religion to transform itself from theology into a science of religions that can "remove historic incrustations" from dogma and worship, and confront spontaneous religious constructions with the results of natural science.[38] It can discriminate the common and the essential from the individual and local elements of religious beliefs. Those beliefs can then be tested in the different ways in which any beliefs are tested, including by the consequences that follow from acting on them. But it is not possible to remove historic encrustations from dogma and worship and still understand, explain, and assess the consequences of those doctrines and practices. James's description of the piety of St. Teresa and the mysticism of Meister Eckhart seem inadequate because they are not adequately illumined by historical context. Nor is it possible to differentiate the common and essential from individual and local elements of religious beliefs. Such a differentiation always depends on the aims of a particular inquiry. James recognizes this at the outset of *Varieties* when he refuses to provide an essentialist definition of religion. Instead, he offers an account of what he means by the term "for the purpose of these lectures."[39]

James's fears about the consequences of a world in which naturalistic explanations were sufficient might have been somewhat allayed by attention to the historical origins of the powers that make for righteousness and for evil in the world. Attention to history could also have provided a richer account than James's metaphysical pluralism gives of the multiple moral resources that are available to people. If James had allowed, with Nietzsche, that the various moral orders to which his sources testify are the products of history, he would have enriched his pluralist account and prepared the way for a better understanding of religious beliefs and practices. The "more" that is, in his words, continuous with the higher parts of the self and operative in the universe outside it, is the product of the desires, imaginations, and actions of men and women, and it is a force available for both good and bad. This order consists of ideas, social practices, and institutions, many of which may be unseen in the sense that we are not conscious of the ways in which they shape actions and the world. A historical naturalism would have the advantage of bringing this unseen order into a realm in which we could inquire about its character and consequences, and even try to alter it.

I call this an advantage. James would not have called it that. For him, and for those whose experience he examines, the "more" that is the object of religious belief is not a historical product, and that is what offers hope. He has already given up the idea of a guarantee. A historical naturalism would require him to give up his conviction, or his hope, that there are forces in the universe, apart from what human beings have put there, that are continuous with the higher parts of the self. Moral ideals, and any forces in the universe that might contribute to their realization, are the product of history and the development of culture, including religion.

The naturalism James found so threatening, and that worried him about the direction he thought some scientists and devotees of science were taking, was identical with materialism and determinism. That's the naturalism depicted in the image of the frozen lake with the melting ice. For him, it meant a world devoid of any promise or hope of change. In *Pragmatism* he writes strikingly that the terms "God," "free will," and "Spirit" all mean the same thing, and that is the presence of promise in the world.[40]

Without this, all would be determined, we would be condemned to our present fate, and there would be no novelty. But with a sufficiently historical understanding of human life and of the resources for and causes of human action, one can allow for imagination, choice, and novelty. These provide for the possibility of change, without a guarantee, and that's the conclusion at which James himself arrives. Without the identification of naturalism with determinism, the possibility of a fully natural explanation of our moral resources need not present us with the fatalism James expresses in his image of the community stranded on the melting ice.

In thinking about the making of knowledge, James realizes that language, social practices, and institutions are human creations and can be modified to fit new tasks, but he thinks that the moral resources we need go beyond this, and that religious experience offers hope for something more. When we recognize that the only resources with which we have to work and that are shaped to our ideals are historical products, it becomes possible to think of altering them for the better. This is seldom simple, it cannot always be done, and it can never be done in such a way that we can fully predict and control the consequences. But study of religion, like the study of other aspects of culture, might help provide some critical leverage on these problems.

NOTES

I want to thank Ann Taves and Philip Kitcher for their comments at the conference.

1. William James, *The Varieties of Religious Experience* (Cambridge: Harvard University Press, 1985), 51.

2. William James, *Pragmatism* (Cambridge: Harvard University Press, 1985), 264.

3. William James, *The Will to Believe* (Cambridge: Harvard University Press, 1979), 84, 70.

4. For James, see the first six essays in *The Will to Believe*; for Nietzsche, *On the Genealogy of Morality*, tr. Maudemarie Clark and Alan J. Swenson (Indianapolis: Hackett, 1998), and *The Anti-Christ*, in *Twilight of the Idols/The Anti-Christ*, tr. R. J. Hollingdale (Harmondsworth, England: Penguin, 1968).

5. Nietzsche, *The Anti-Christ*, 136–137.

6. Friedrich Nietzsche, *The Gay Science*, tr. Josefine Nauckhoff and Adrian Del Caro (Cambridge: Cambridge University Press, 2001), 202 (V, 346).

7. Matthew Arnold, *Literature and Dogma* (New York: Macmillan, 1902), 52.

8. *The Correspondence of William James*, 10 vols., ed. Ignas K. Skrupskelis and Elizabeth M. Berkeley (Charlottesville: University of Virginia Press, 1992), 5:195.

9. James, *Varieties*, 120.

10. James, *The Will to Believe*, 54.

11. James, *Varieties*, 523.

12. James, *Pragmatism*, 264.

13. James, *Varieties*, 45–46.

14. Ibid. 188.

15. James, *The Principles of Psychology* (Cambridge: Harvard University Press, 1983).

16. James, *Varieties*, 13.

17. Ibid. 25.

18. Ibid. 193.

19. Ibid. 174.

20. Ibid. 188.

21. Ann Taves, *Fits, Trances, and Visions* (Princeton: Princeton University Press, 1999), 253–260. See also "The Fragmentation of Consciousness and *The Varieties of Religious Experience*: William James's Contribution to a Theory of Religion," in this volume, esp. 66–82.

22. James, *Varieties*, 190.

23. Ibid. 192*n*. See also Taves's chapter in this volume.

24. Ibid.

25. Taves notes that for Myers the common feature of automatisms was that they were "message-bearing or nunciative." *Fits, Trances, and Visions*, 236. There was a meaning component.

26. William James, review of Janet, *État mental des hystériques*, and notice of J. Breuer and S. Freud, "Über den psychischen Mechanismus hysterischer Phänomene," *Psychological Review* 1 (March 1894): 195–199.

27. James, *Varieties*, 366–367.

28. Ibid. 400.

29. See David Hollinger's chapter in this volume.

30. James, *Varieties*, 283.

31. Ibid. 277.

32. William James, "Introduction to *The Literary Remains of the Late Henry James*," *Essays in Religion and Morality* (Cambridge: Harvard University Press, 1982), 62.

33. James, *Varieties,* 134–135. See 508 for James's acknowledgment, in a letter to Frank Abauzit, that this account is of his own case.

34. James, *The Will to Believe,* 133.

35. James, *Varieties,* 414.

36. James, *Pragmatism,* 142–143.

37. In the concluding chapter of *Varieties* James tries to maintain a neutral position about the sufficiency of natural explanations for the "more" that is common to religious experiences. In the postscript, carefully distinguished from the conclusions, he opts for a "piecemeal supernaturalism." *Varieties,* 409–410.

38. Ibid. 359.

39. Ibid. 32.

40. James, *Pragmatism,* 61.

3

⸎

The Fragmentation of Consciousness and
The Varieties of Religious Experience
William James's Contribution to a Theory of Religion

ANN TAVES

INTRODUCTION

James structured *The Varieties of Religious Experience* around two large questions about religion: what does it do? (a question of function) and whence does it come? (a question of origins).[1] But, as he made clear in his opening lecture, his central concern was not so much with religion broadly conceived as with the experience of people who could be considered "'geniuses' in the religious line," those whose original experiences set the pattern for others, rather than "ordinary religious believers" whose religion was made by others, communicated through tradition, and maintained by habit.[2] The deeper question that informed the question of origins for James was whether the claims of such exceptional people could be "literally and objectively true." Were these individuals literally and objectively "moved by an external power"—in the context of prayer, prophecy, inspiration, or visionary experience—or not?[3] His question was not simply whether such experiences had value for life, but rather whether they could be understood as true in relationship with "other truths that also have to be acknowledged."[4]

In *Varieties*, James offered a theoretical explanation of how people might experience a sense of an external presence of something they take to be divine that was congruent, in his view, with the various truths—experiential, theological, and scientific—that he felt needed to be acknowledged. His theoretical explanation rested on an unattributed discovery made in 1886, which he referred to in *Varieties* as "the most important step forward in psychology since [he had] been a student of that science." It revealed, he said, "an entirely unsuspected peculiarity in the constitution of human nature," specifically "that, in certain subjects at least, there is . . . a set of memories, thoughts, and feelings which are extra-marginal and outside the primary consciousness altogether, but yet must be classed as conscious facts of some sort, able to reveal their presence by unmistakable signs."[5] "This discovery of consciousness beyond the field," James argued, "casts light on many phenomena of religious biography."[6] This unattributed discovery and its application to religious experience marks, in my view, an important and underappreciated contribution to discussions of theory and method in the study of religion.

This reading of *Varieties* owes a great debt to Eugene Taylor, whose work on exceptional mental states and consciousness beyond the margin effectively made the case that *Varieties* is a psychological book informed by psychological theory.[7] James scholarship in religious studies owes a similar debt to Wayne Proudfoot, whose book on religious experience brought *Varieties* out of the psychology of religion, where it was regularly honored, if not deeply probed, and into wider philosophical discussions about religious experience.[8] Since then other philosophers of religion, including Grace Jantzen, David Lamberth, and Bill Barnard, have taken up *Varieties* in relation to larger questions in the philosophy and theology of religion.[9] James is rarely cited, however, in contemporary discussions of theory and method. Indeed, David Wulff, author of a leading textbook on the psychology of religion, recently concluded that the influence of *Varieties* was "largely general . . . for in it *James elaborated neither a specific theory nor a particular method*, beyond the judicious use of personal documents."[10]

Since I have attempted elsewhere to dispel the idea that James elaborated neither a theory nor a method, my aim here is to lift up those aspects of his theory and method that I think are most worth recovering. Doing so requires digging into footnotes and allusive references to retrieve his conversation partners in the field of experimental psychology and psychical research. I will begin by using the unattributed discovery of 1886, which in my view has been consistently misinterpreted, to illuminate the experimental and theoretical underpinnings of *Varieties*. In the process, I will lift up both the comparative method and the experimentally based theory of the self that informed James's work. Approaching *Varieties* in this fashion allows us to specify more clearly the kinds of experience that interested James. This in turn circumscribes his explanation of religious experience and, in my view, makes it more compelling.

My approach to the text is admittedly partial, but not, I think, unfair to James's aims in writing *The Varieties of Religious Experience*. James was a psychologist, a philosopher, and a metaphysician at a time when those roles were not always sharply distinguished. *Varieties* can be read from any of these vantage points. In the book, however, he also took on the role of scientist of religion, whose task, as he saw it, was to formulate a hypothesis about religion to which "physical science need not object." In this role, he operated within a set of self-imposed constraints in an effort to come up with a theory of religious experience that was faithful to the experience of believers, the phenomenological contentions of the theologians, and the plausibility structures of the scientists. Only in the final pages of the book does he go beyond this to admit to his own "overbeliefs."[11] While some (e.g., Lamberth and Barnard) want to reread *Varieties* without these constraints so as to get a fuller picture of James's own metaphysical views, I am content in this context to leave them in place.

THE EXPERIMENTAL EVIDENCE FOR SECONDARY SELVES

A fuller understanding of James's theory of religious experience must begin with an unpacking of what he meant by "consciousness beyond the field," and we can't understand that without knowing whom he was crediting with its discovery. Most James scholars, including Eugene Taylor, have concluded, with little or no compelling evidence, that James was referring to Frederick Myers, one of the founders of the British Society for Psychical Research.[12] Without diminishing the importance of Myers's work for James, there is substantial evidence to suggest that James was referring to the French experimental psychologist, Pierre Janet, whose first published report of his experiments with the "hysterical somnambule," Léonie, appeared in 1886, and not to Frederick Myers.[13] In their exegesis

of the James passage, scholars have confused James's appropriation of
Myers's particular understanding of the subconscious with the discovery
of co-conscious "secondary selves" that undergirded Myers's theory. This
basic discovery, which James silently attributed to Pierre Janet in *Varieties*
and, in other contexts, to Janet, Edmund Gurney, and Alfred Binet, was
the distinguishing feature of what Alan Gauld has referred to as the
"golden age of the subconscious."[14]

While there is evidence to suggest that Myers anticipated Janet's discovery and that indeed Janet was aware of and drew upon Myers's work,
I am less interested in questions of precedence than in clearly identifying
the basic discovery to which James was referring. Specifically, I want to
suggest that James was referring to the discovery of simultaneously *coex-
istent* states of consciousness, referred to by Janet and Myers as "*secondary* selves," as opposed to *alternating* (i.e., non-coexistent) personalities,
which were widely discussed in the earlier era of animal magnetism.
Janet, according to both Myers and James, provided the first widely acknowledged experimental evidence for such secondary selves in his 1886
article.[15]

Myers *did* to some extent anticipate Janet's findings on the basis of his
and Gurney's work with telepathy and automatic writing.[16] In an article
published in 1885 and cited by Janet in 1886, Myers recognized the limits
of the older theory of "unconscious cerebration" for explaining the case
of "Clelia," a spiritualist medium.[17] In her, he observed a "kind of active
duality of mentation," a "colloquy between a conscious and an unconscious self." He referred to the second center of consciousness as "[a] *secondary self*," which he defined as "a latent capacity, . . . in an appreciable
fraction of mankind, of developing or manifesting a second focus of cerebral energy which . . . may possess, for a time at least, a kind of continuous individuality, a purposive activity of its own."[18] Based on Myers's 1885
article, which Janet cited in 1886, Nathan Hale concluded that Janet got
the idea of a secondary self from Myers.[19]

Nonetheless, Myers did not see the Clelia case or the somewhat similar observations he made in a note appended to *Phantasms of the Living*
(1886) as the point where his basic understanding of the self took shape.
Rather, in his introduction to his posthumously published *Human Personality*, Myers indicated that "this conclusion [his basic understanding
of the self] . . . assumed for me something like its present shape some

fourteen years since," i.e., in 1887.[20] Myers (or his editors) cited in this regard an article on "Automatic Writing," published in January 1887, much
of which was devoted to the evidence put forth by Janet in his 1886 article and in an unpublished manuscript, which Janet had shown to him
(246). In his 1887 article, Myers credited Janet with "discover[ing] a
method by which, in an exceptionally sensitive subject, hypnotic writing,
prolonged by suggestion into the normal state, could be made into a
means of communication with the hypnotic self, *coincidentally* with ordinary verbal intercourse with the waking self" (236; emphasis added). According to Myers, Janet's experiments with Léonie, the subject of his 1886
article, "mark the highest degree yet obtained of proof of the origination
of automatic writing in the recesses of the writer's own identity" (236).

With the publication in 1887 of experiments conducted by Edmund
Gurney, Myers's colleague in the British S.P.R., Myers and James began
giving credit to both Gurney and Janet when they summed up the experimental evidence for secondary selves. In *Principles*, James wrote:

> The experiments of Gurney and the observations of M. Pierre Janet
> and others on certain hysterical somnambulists seem to prove that it
> [the post-hypnotic suggestion] is stored up in consciousness; not
> simply organically registered, but that *the consciousness which thus
> retains it is split off, dissociated from the rest of the author's mind.* We
> have here, in short, an experimental production of one of those "sec-
> ond" states of personality of which we have spoken so often. Only
> here the second state coexists as well as alternates with the first.[21]

Inspired by Janet's research, Gurney, according to James, had "the brilliant idea of *tapping* this second consciousness [in normal subjects] by
means of the planchette," the Ouija board-like device used by spiritualists
to spell out words.[22] Gurney himself described his experiments as novel,
"though tame and rudimentary enough, compared with the only hither-
to recorded case to which they seem at all akin—the dramatic self-
duplication of Prof. Janet's patient." He added that "they present at any
rate this advantage, that they had no connection with hysterical conditions, but were conducted with normal healthy 'subjects.'"[23]

In later references, James added Alfred Binet's name to Janet's and
Gurney's when referring to the experimental evidence for the splitting of
consciousness. Binet, whose *Les altérations de la personnalité* appeared in

1892, extended Janet's work on hysterical subjects while at the same time including chapters on "the plurality of consciousness in healthy subjects" and the "division of personality and spiritism."[24] It was perhaps because Binet's volume effectively linked Janet's experiments with hysterical subjects and Gurney's with healthy ones that James recommended it to readers of *Varieties* desiring an account of the evidence upon which the idea of a "consciousness existing beyond the field" was based.[25]

In "What Psychical Research Has Accomplished" (1892) and later in *The Will to Believe* (1896), James again credited Janet, Gurney, and Binet with "demonstrating the simultaneous existence of two different strata of consciousness, ignorant of each other, in the same person." But in the latter he added, *"This discovery marks a new era in experimental psychology, and it is impossible to overrate its importance."*[26] It was this new era that Janet inaugurated in 1886 when he published the first experimental evidence of the simultaneous existence of two strata of consciousness.

THE FRAGMENTED SELF: NORMAL OR PATHOLOGICAL?

The idea of secondary selves or strata of consciousness, which this new research claimed to demonstrate, was premised on the notion that consciousness was divisible. Janet referred to this as the *désagrégation* of consciousness, James as the splitting off or dissociation of portions of consciousness.[27] Those who accepted the dissociative model of consciousness understood the self or selves in relation to "chains of memory." While memories were "associated" within a chain, they were "dissociated" between chains. Through hypnosis, researchers engaged (and created) chains of memory that were dissociated from the chain of memory that constituted the person's usual sense of self.[28] The new theory, in effect, postulated that chains of bodily memories, if sufficiently extensive and elaborate, could in turn constitute distinct selves or personalities. These dissociated memory chains, which could be tapped and extended by means of hypnosis and automatic writing, offered a theoretical model whereby two "selves" could coexist in one body.

While Janet, Binet, Gurney, Myers, and James all presupposed a dissociative model of consciousness, they disagreed about the conditions under which the splitting of consciousness could occur. Janet, who followed his mentor, the neurologist Jean-Martin Charcot, on this point, viewed all manifestations of a secondary self as symptomatic of hysteria and thus as inherently pathological. He stood apart from Binet, Gurney, Myers, and James, who, like Charcot's rivals at Nancy, believed that secondary centers of consciousness could exist in healthy people.[29] While they all accepted the evidence for the dissociation or splitting of consciousness, they disagreed on what it meant for understanding the self. The basic question was whether "all the phenomena of hypnotism, double consciousness, &c.," as Myers put it, could be explained "as mere morbid disaggregations of the empirical personality."[30] Was the healthy mind unified and the diseased mind divided, as Janet maintained? Or was the mind, as Myers was to conclude, naturally "multiplex"?

THE MULTIPLEX PERSONALITY

Myers's primary contribution to the experimental psychology of the subconscious was not, in James's view, as an experimental researcher but as a theorist. His theory of the subliminal consciousness, as James noted, provided the chief alternative to Janet's theory of pathological mental *désagregation*.[31] Although James was convinced that secondary centers of consciousness could exist in healthy people by his observations of the spiritualist medium, Leonora Piper, and his participation in the census of hallucinations conducted by the S.P.R., Myers developed a theory to account for this evidence.

Automatic Writing

Myers developed his theory of the multiplex self from the same basic ideas as Pierre Janet: secondary personalities, chains of memory, and automatic writing. Where Myers began with cases of spontaneous automatic writing reported by Spiritualists and other presumptively healthy people, Janet began with patients diagnosed as hysterics and induced automatic writing by means of hypnosis. Myers's essays on automatic writing unfold, as Sonu Shamdasani points out, around the question of "Who writes?"[32] Myers pursued this question in his 1887 article using a detailed account of a series of Spiritualist-style experiments with the planchette conducted by the Oxford philosopher F. C. S. Schiller and his siblings. Schiller commented on what he took to be the "more remarkable points" in his report to Myers, without, however, endorsing either the

"Spiritualist explanation" or the "'unconscious-self' theory."[33] In his article, Myers compared Schiller's spontaneous examples of automatic writing with the automatic writing produced in response to hypnotic suggestion by Janet's patient, Léonie. Where "a new and separate invading personality" might have been assumed in spontaneously occurring cases of automatic writing, it was clear, Myers wrote, that in the case of Léonie "the 'communicating intelligence' was of so obviously artificial a kind that it could scarcely venture to pretend to be either a devil or Louise's [Léonie's dead] grandmother."[34] Janet, in other words, was able to demonstrate what until that time could only be inferred: that what seemed subjectively to come from outside the self could originate "in the recesses of the writer's own identity."[35] In light of this and other comparisons, Myers felt that "the apparent uniqueness of such a phenomenon as the Schiller messages—the apparent externality of the dictating intelligence,— . . . [grew] fainter and more questionable." He did not, however, conclude from this that the automatic writing was necessarily "something morbid, retrograde, or hysterical."[36]

In contrast to Janet, who was primarily interested in treating mental illness, Myers, like other psychical researchers, was motivated by an interest in human evolution and the evidence for supranormal phenomena such as clairvoyance, telepathy, or communication with discarnate spirits that might be associated with it. In keeping with this broader aim, he insisted "that each case of apparent automatism should be considered simply on its own merits, without being supposed to imply either disease or inspiration."[37] Methodologically, he was convinced that

if we are to understand supernormal phenomena—phenomena transcending, apparently, the state of evolution at which we have admittedly arrived,—we must first compare them, as fully as possible, both with normal and with abnormal phenomena. . . . [Moreover] we must expect that supernormal phenomena, if they occur at all, will show many points of resemblance to abnormal—nay, to positively morbid—phenomena, without therefore themselves necessarily deserving to be classed as morbid in any degree. When unfamiliar impulses arise in the organism—whether these impulses be evolutive or dissolutive in character—their readiest paths of externalisation are likely to be somewhat similar.[38]

As the S.P.R.'s premier theorist, he may have pioneered this approach. He, at least, felt it was novel, admitting that he could not find it "set forth in any accredited textbook."[39] It is also quite clearly the approach that James adopted in *Varieties*. He acknowledged at the outset that the religious virtuosos, or, in his words, the "'geniuses' in the religious line" that interested him were often "subject to abnormal psychical visitations." Like Myers, James claimed "we [could] not possibly ignore these pathological elements of the subject." He provided a long excursus attacking medical materialism in order to assure his listeners that "the bugaboo of morbid origin" need not "scandalize [their] piety." Indeed, like Myers, he suspected that "if there were such a thing as inspiration from a higher realm," the "neurotic temperament" might furnish "the chief condition" for receiving it. Perhaps most notably, James believed that his wide-ranging comparisons were the distinguishing feature of his lectures. At the conclusion of his first one, he stated outright that "the only novelty that I can imagine this course of lectures to possess lies in the breadth of the apperceiving mass," that is, "the mass of collateral phenomena, morbid or healthy, with which the various religious phenomena must be compared in order to understand them better."[40]

Myers's conviction that the normal mind is multiplex grew out of, on the one hand, his interest in potentially supernormal phenomena, and on the other, his need to account for the unusual experiences associated with automatic writing reported by presumptively normal people. "The graphic automatist [e.g., Spiritualist medium] tells us of insurgent quasi-personalities,—not momentary, but of indefinite persistence . . . susceptible of considerable multiplication, as one new 'guide' or 'control' is added to another, without appreciably disturbing the ordinary current of life." But, he added, "we have seen that this fissiparous multiplication of the self,—if I may so term it—is by no means so rare a phenomenon as has sometimes been supposed."[41] Generalizing from the cases—normal and pathological—that he had examined, he suggested that "whenever there is any habitual alteration, physiological or pathological, of the threshold of consciousness we shall find an incipient formation of a secondary chain of memories, linking together those periods of altered consciousness into a series of their own. And when once a second mnemonic chain is woven, the emergence of a secondary personality is only a matter of degree."[42]

Two years later, he elaborated on this point, theorizing that "each of us contain the potentialities of many different arrangements of the elements of our personality, each arrangement being distinguishable from the rest by differences in the chain of memories which pertains to it." The "normal or primary self . . . with which we habitually identify ourselves" consisted, according to Myers, of that part of the self selected (in the evolutionary sense) for its fitness in dealing with our "ordinary physical needs." He did not view it as "necessarily superior in any other respect to the latent personalities which lie along side it." Moreover, he said, "we can at present assign no limit . . . [to] the fresh combinations of our personal elements that may be evoked by accident or design." A variety of normal and pathological phenomena, according to Myers, might evoke such fresh combinations. Thus, he said, "dreams, with natural somnambulism, automatic writing, with so-called mediumistic trance, as well as certain intoxications, epilepsies, hysterias, and recurrent insanities, afford examples of the development of what I have called secondary mnemonic chains,—fresh personalities, more or less complete, alongside the normal state."

Automatisms

The concept of the automatism provided Myers with the crucial theoretical link between the S.P.R.'s experiments on automatic writing and Janet's research on hysteria. Working by analogy, Myers argued in 1889 that "automatic writing is but one among a whole series of kindred automatisms which have been intermittently noted, divergently interpreted, since history began."[43] According to James, his was "the first attempt in our language, and the first thoroughly *inductive* attempt in any language, to consider the phenomena of hallucination, hypnotism, automatism, double personality, and mediumship as connected parts of one whole subject. No one seems to me to have grasped the problem in a way both so broad and so sober as he has done."[44] James later referred to this as a "great simplification" that in one stroke placed "hallucinations and active impulses under a common head, as *sensory* and *motor automatisms*."[45]

Although he used "automatisms" as a unifying conceptual term, he specified the common feature that the term was meant to suggest. "The positive bond of connection" between the various sorts of automatisms, the "quality common to them all," according to Myers, was their "message-bearing or nunciative" character. Subjectively, these messages—whether "verbalization, picture, motor impulse, or other impression"—come to consciousness "*as though from some extraneous source,*—it is presented as *an automatic product whose initiation lies outside the conscious will.*" They suggest, Myers adds, "that some strain of intelligence, whether without us or within, *which is not our conscious waking intelligence of the moment,* is in some fashion impressing or informing the conscious self." "Originating [most often] in some deeper zone of a man's being," he said, "they float up into superficial consciousness as deeds, visions, words, ready-made and full-blown, without any accompanying perception of the elaborate process which has made them what they are."[46]

As Myers expanded his theory from automatic writing to automatisms, he bolstered his argument against a purely pathological interpretation of such experiences by including both everyday and historically significant examples. Dreams, he argued, could be regarded as the "commonest form of message-bearing automatisms; that is to say, they are phenomena, whose origin is within ourselves, but yet outside our habitual stream of consciousness." Explicitly shying away from the more controversial cases of "religious fanaticism or ecstacy" that James would later embrace, Myers lifted up Socrates—"the Founder of Science himself,—the permanent type of sanity, shrewdness, physical robustness, and moral balance,—[who] was guided in all the affairs of life by a monitory Voice"—and Joan of Arc, "the national heroine of France," as historical figures guided by voices or visions, whose sanity no one was willing to question.[47]

Automatisms, the primary means of communication between the subliminal and supraliminal levels of consciousness in Myers's fully developed theory of the self, played a central role in the religious biographies James examined in *Varieties*. Where Myers avoided religious examples as too controversial, James took George Fox as his exemplary case, acknowledging up front that, despite his spiritual soundness, he was "from the point of view of his nervous constitution, . . . a psychopath or détraqué of the deepest dye" (15–16). "In point of fact," he argued in his penultimate lecture, you will "hardly find a religious leader of any kind in whose life there is no record of automatisms." He added that he was not referring simply to "savage priests and prophets," but to "the whole array of Christian saints and heresiarchs, including the greatest, the Bernards, the Loyolas, the Luthers, the Foxes, the Wesleys, [all of whom] had their visions, voices, rapt conditions, guiding impressions, and 'openings'" (376–377).

Subliminal Consciousness

Myers unfolded his own fully developed alternative to Janet's theory of pathological *désagrégation* in a series entitled "The Subliminal Consciousness," published in *Proceedings* between 1892 and 1894. Many of the central ideas had already appeared in his earlier articles on automatic writing and in his reviews of the French research. His explicit aim in these essays was to construct an alternative to the explanations of the French schools at Paris (hysteria) and Nancy (suggestion) by bringing together the research on hypnotic trance, automatic writing, alternations of personality, telepathy, and clairvoyance.[48] He summarized his alternative theory in a much-quoted paragraph:

> I suggest, then, that the stream of consciousness in which we habitually live is not the only consciousness which exists in connection with our organism. Our habitual or empirical consciousness may consist of a mere selection from a multitude of thoughts and sensations, of which some at least are equally conscious with those that we empirically know. I accord no primacy to my ordinary waking self, except that among my potential selves this one has shown itself the fittest to meet the needs of common life. I hold that it has established no further claim, and that it is perfectly possible that other thoughts, feelings, and memories, either isolated or in continuous connection, may now be actively conscious, as we say, "within me,"—in some kind of co-ordination with my organism, and forming some part of my total individuality.[49]

Two developments are worth highlighting: his change in terminology and his expanded understanding of the ways in which messages might manifest themselves. First, with respect to the terminology, Myers settled on "subliminal" and "supraliminal" as a more adequate way to refer to what he had been calling secondary and primary selves. "Subliminal" referred to all the "psychical action" occurring "below the threshold of our habitual consciousness" and "supraliminal" to the habitual consciousness (or the "empirical self"). To refer to the "subliminal" as the "unconscious," or even 'subconscious,'" he said, "would be directly misleading; and to speak (as is sometimes convenient) of the *secondary* self may give the impression either that there cannot be more than two, or that the *supraliminal* self, the self above the threshold,—the empirical self, the self of common experience—is in some way superior to other possible selves."[50] Second, as his theory developed, Myers's understanding of "message-bearing" phenomena expanded. In his earliest essays, he focused on automatic writing; in 1889, he turned to automatisms more generally; and, in 1892, he described four modes of manifestation, which included and went beyond automatisms narrowly defined. As of 1892, he described messages as falling into four broad categories: "vague or anomalous impressions or impulses" that were neither definitely sensory nor definitely motor; sensory messages (visual or auditory hallucinations); motor messages (speaking, writing, gestures); and "messages at once motor and sensory, which tend to occupy the whole psychical field, and to pass on into states of trance, or of alternating personality."[51] The two most familiar examples of the second and fourth modes were, he said, dreams and sleep. In dreams, we have "at once the weakest and the commonest form of sensory hallucination." In sleep, "we have . . . a first familiar example of that shifting of the strata of personality" wherein "the subliminal self may displace the supraliminal."[52]

We can, at this point, highlight certain distinctive features of Myers's understanding of the subliminal consciousness or self that derived from the research on secondary selves. First, "'The Subliminal Self' is a name for *an aggregate of potential personalities*, with imperfectly known capacities of perception and action." Defining it thus, Myers is better understood as claiming that we have a *capacity* to develop or manifest such personalities than as depicting them as a permanent feature of the subliminal self. The self, as conceived by Myers, was fissiparous. Second, he indicated that, since these personalities may emerge and develop and then disappear, they do not have the characteristics that philosophers usually ascribe to "an incorporeal soul." Third, the subliminal self could be implicated in both pathological and supranormal phenomena. In emphasizing the possibility that supranormal phenomena such as ecstasy and genius might manifest through the subliminal self, Myers did not mean to suggest that "the subliminal self is free from disturbance and disease." Rather, his intent was to free both hypnotism and the aggregate of subliminal (formerly, secondary) selves from the purely pathological interpretation attributed to them by Janet.[53]

Myers's theory of the subliminal self provided a new psychological framework for understanding a wide range of phenomena, including many religious phenomena, without reducing them to epiphenomena of psychopathology or necessarily ruling out influences beyond the self. When Myers began formulating his theory, he recognized that his explanation of the "trance of the automatist" was "by no means identical" with that of the Spiritualists, "who say that the writing medium is 'mesmerized by the controlling Spirit.'" He added, however, that "in putting forward this new explanation, which refers the trance to a mere change of cerebral equilibrium—a mere shifting of the psychical centre of energy within the personality of the automatist himself,—I do not mean to deny the possibility that some influence external to the writer's may at times be operative."[54] By placing the pathological, the normal, and the potentially supranormal within a common frame of reference, Myers created a theoretical space (the subliminal) through which influences beyond the individual, should they exist, might be expected to manifest themselves. In explaining spirit possession as a "shifting of the psychical center of energy *within the personality of the automatist himself*" without ruling out "the possibility that *some influence external* to the [automatist] may at times be operative," Myers modeled the open-ended approach to explanation that James later adopted in *Varieties*.

As Wayne Proudfoot has argued, "the sense of the presence of an unseen reality [is] the thread that runs through the *Varieties* . . . [and] the common denominator of the experiences that James considers."[55] In his famous description of the "uneasiness and its solution," James locates the transformative power of this unseen reality at the heart of religion in general. We are saved, he says, from the sense that "there is something wrong about us . . . by making a proper connection with the higher powers," with, that is, the unseen reality that he goes on to call the "More." It is the "unseen reality" of the "More," and the potentially transformative power of engagement with it, that James sought to explain theoretically in *Varieties*.

In formulating an explanation, James sought, as a scientist of religion, to avoid the particularistic vocabularies of the theologians and "to keep religion in connection with the rest of science." In order to do so, he said, "we shall do well to seek first of all a way of describing the 'more,' which psychologists may also recognize as real."[56] Claiming that "the *subconscious self* is nowadays a well-accredited psychological entity," he turned to it as "the mediating term required," explicitly equating it with the subliminal consciousness of Myers's 1892 essay. Building on what he took to be the "recognized psychological fact" of the subconscious, James "propose[d], as an hypothesis, that whatever it may be on its *farther* side, the 'more' with which in religious experience we feel ourselves connected is on its *hither* side the subconscious continuation of our conscious life."

This hypothesis had two key features, according to James: "we seem to preserve a contact with 'science' which the ordinary theologian lacks. At the same time the theologian's contention that the religious man is moved by an external power is vindicated, for it is one of the peculiarities of invasions from the subconscious region *to take on objective appearances*, and *to suggest to the Subject* an external control" (403–404). This last sentence is interesting and potentially misleading. Taken as a whole, it makes clear that the theologian's contention is not vindicated epistemologically, as Barnard claims, but simply phenomenologically.[57] Invasions from the subconscious *seem* objective and *suggest to the subject* an external control. James is not endorsing the theologian's truth claims here; he is offering a theoretical explanation of how individuals might subjectively experience a presence that they take to be an external power, when such is not necessarily the case. Although James did not rule out the possibility of higher powers that were truly outside the self, in his view it is "*primarily* the higher faculties of our own hidden mind which are controlling."[58]

James's reliance on Myers and Janet reframes our understanding of *Varieties* at three key points. First, as just noted, he explained the religious person's experience of an unseen presence in terms of the subliminal or subconscious self. All the varieties of religious experience that he considered—conversion, inspiration, sainthood, and mysticism—demonstrate, as he put it, "that in religion we have a department of human nature with unusually close relations to the transmarginal or subliminal region."[59] Second, in linking religious experience with the subliminal, he located it as part of the "one whole subject" constituted by hallucination, hypnotism, automatism, double personality, and mediumship. For James, the act of locating religious experience within this broad comparative framework was the distinguishing feature of his lectures.[60] Third, his frame of reference, while broadly comparative, left room for religious belief. Indeed, for James the real beauty of Myers's (as opposed to Janet's) understanding of the subconscious was that it ultimately said very little about origins. In adopting Myers's conception, James left open the question of where the subconscious ended, whether in the personal self or beyond it, and thus placed *ultimate* questions about origins outside the purview of the science of religions.[61] Although James was willing to account for most experiences of an unseen reality in terms of the "higher powers of our own hidden mind," his open-ended understanding of the subconscious allowed for other possibilities as well. We are left then with a theory that is intended to explain much, but not necessarily all, of what James took to be religious experience in terms of shifting psychical centers of energy within a self that is understood to be inherently fissiparous.

THE THEORETICAL AND METHODOLOGICAL CONTRIBUTIONS OF *VARIETIES* TO THE SOCIAL SCIENTIFIC STUDY OF RELIGION

While the importance of the subconscious or subliminal in James's theory of religion has not escaped most readers, both the experimental evidence and the comparative methodology that informed it have largely been lost.[62] Reconstructing this aspect of James's thought through the writings of Janet and Myers highlights the following points with respect to the contemporary study of religious experience:

1. Comparison between religious and nonreligious phenomena is crucial for the construction of theories of religion. Recognition of the methodological underpinnings of *Varieties* locates James, along with Myers, as pioneers of a form of comparison between religious and nonreligious phenomena not usually embraced by scholars of religion. We should pay greater heed to Myers's methodological dictum: "if we are to understand supernormal phenomena . . . we must first compare them, as fully as possible, both with normal and with abnormal phenomena." While Myers's questions may differ from ours, his dictum still carries weight. Limiting our comparisons to phenomena we deem religious at the outset can function as a protective strategy, insofar as it obscures contestations over what counts as religion. Openness to considering contested phenomena, such as the unusual experiences studied by James, and openness to comparing experiences understood as religious

with experiences understood as nonreligious or even pathological, as advocated by Myers, allows us to explore the construction (and deconstruction) of religious experiences and thus the construction and deconstruction of religion as a category. Such work is inherently interdisciplinary and is one way, as William Paden has pointed out, to help "reestablish the connection that has been lacking between religious studies and the other human sciences."[63]

2. Through the appropriation of Myers's notion of the subliminal/subconscious, James was able to offer a theoretical explanation of religious experiences that located them on a continuum with the "ordinary phenomena of mental dissociation," without necessarily reducing them to psychopathology or ruling out influences beyond the individual.[64] James moved beyond Myers, not in terms of theory or method, but in terms of his interest in religious experience *per se* and, consequently, in terms of the range of religious phenomena—conversion, inspiration, saintliness, and mysticism—that he brought under the theoretical umbrella Myers had constructed. This was a crucial move on James's part and one that can rightly be criticized.[65] The central problem, I would argue, is not with locating some forms of experience that some would consider religious on a continuum with ordinary phenomena of mental dissociation, but with defining religious experience in such a way that it is explained, quite circularly, by the theory one has set out to propound. This problem, of course, is endemic in the theoretical literature on religion.[66]

3. The theoretical contributions of Myers and James are more evident (and more circumscribed) if we highlight the features that the experiences they compared had in common. In Jonathan Smith's well-known words, comparison by definition "lifts out and strongly marks certain features within difference as being of possible intellectual significance, expressed in the rhetoric of their being 'like' in some stipulated fashion." Smith emphasizes the scholar's agency in this process. "Comparison," he stresses, "provides the means by which we 're-vision' phenomena as *our* data in order to solve *our* theoretical problems."[67] Myers and James lifted out similar features of the phenomena they were comparing. The key feature for Myers was that of messages coming to consciousness "as though from some extraneous source"; for James, it was the subjective sense of being "moved by an external power." They both attempted to explain experiences in which the subject's sense of agency was altered or ab-

sent. Both articulated what the experiences had in common from the perspective of the experiencer, even though they did not necessarily think
their subjects' explanations of their experiences were correct. Clearly articulating what a set of experiences has in common is crucial if we want
to avoid overgeneralization. Articulating what a set of experiences has in
common *from the standpoint of the experiencer*, as Wayne Proudfoot has
argued, is crucial if we want to avoid descriptive reductionism.

4. Myers's conception of the self as multiplex provides an important
theoretical lens for understanding religious claims that involve a subjective sense of being moved by an external power. In explaining the experience of an external power in terms of the subconscious/subliminal self,
James adopted an open-ended view of the self and relegated ultimate
questions of causality to the realm of what he called "over-beliefs." James
viewed over-beliefs as "indispensable" and willingly offered his own view
that there is indeed a "mystical region" at the "further limits of our being"
(405). James obviously also thought that specific over-beliefs could be
tested experimentally, as he demonstrated through his involvement with
the Society for Psychical Research and his experiments with Mrs. Piper.
In offering the subconscious as a penultimate explanation, he left the ultimate interpretation of any specific instance of feeling moved by an external power open—to dogmatic assertion, pragmatic testing, or scientific investigation. In doing so, he enshrined what Stewart Guthrie has
referred to as the chronic ambiguity of the perceptual world at the heart
of his theory.[68]

5. Finally, Myers's conception of the self as not simply multiplex but
"fissiparous" provides a point of connection with wider conversations on
the instability of identity and the fragmentation of the self in various contexts, including religionists' discussions of taking on multiple roles or
identities in relation to the people or practices they study, sociological
discussions of the effects of modernity on the self, and controversies over
the authenticity of recovered memories in situations of abuse. The concept of the capacity to create and dissolve alternate "personalities" with
associated chains of memory strikes me as theoretically rich, especially if
we place the more sharply dissociated notion of "personalities" on a continuum with the more common, weakly dissociated experiences of multiple identities, roles, and voices. The idea of the fissiparous self seems especially powerful when embedded socially in relation to the demands of

negotiating the multiple, fragmented communities of discourse and practice that characterize the contemporary world.

NOTES

1. For a discussion of his overall argument, see Ann Taves, *Fits, Trances and Visions: Experiencing Religion and Explaining Experience from Wesley to James* (Princeton: Princeton University Press, 1999), 271–291.

2. William James, *The Varieties of Religious Experience* (Cambridge: Harvard University Press, 1985), 15.

3. Ibid. 405, 403; see also 401, where he asks, "what is the objective truth of their content?" According to James, "the word 'truth' is here taken to mean something additional to bare value for life" (401*n*).

4. In his later essays on pragmatism, James distinguished between two levels of truth. Speaking of theology, he said, "*if theological ideas prove to have a value for concrete life, they will be true, for pragmatism, in the sense of being good for so much. For how much more they are true, will depend entirely on their relation to the other truths that also have to be acknowledged.*" *Pragmatism* (New York: Library of America, 1987), 519. I infer from his overall argument in *Varieties* that in this context he was inquiring about truth in this second sense.

5. James, *Varieties*, 190.

6. Ibid.

7. Eugene Taylor, *William James on Exceptional Mental States* (Amherst: University of Massachusetts Press, 1984); *William James on Consciousness Beyond the Margins* (Princeton: Princeton University Press, 1996); *Shadow Culture: Psychology and Spirituality in America* (Washington: Counterpoint, 1999), 176–182. A number of related studies have also contributed; see, for example: Michael G. Kenny, *The Passion of Ansel Bourne: Multiple Personality in American Culture* (Washington: Smithsonian Institution Press, 1986); Theodore Flournoy, *From India to the Planet Mars: A Case of Multiple Personality with Imaginary Languages,* ed. Sonu Shamdasani (Princeton: Princeton University Press, 1994); and Ian Hacking, *Rewriting the Soul: Multiple Personality and the Sciences of Memory* (Princeton: Princeton University Press, 1995).

8. Wayne Proudfoot, *Religious Experience* (Berkeley: University of California Press, 1985), xvii, 156–157. Proudfoot notes that "*Varieties* has been widely read and commented upon, but its significance for contemporary issues in the philosophy of religion has often been overlooked" (xvii).

9. Grace M. Jantzen, "Mysticism and Experience," *Religious Studies* 25 (1989): 295–315; G. William Barnard, *Exploring Unseen Worlds: William James and the Philosophy of Mysticism* (Albany: SUNY Press, 1997), 7, 170–179; G. William Barnard, "William James and the Origins of Mystical Experience," in *The Innate Capacity,* ed. Robert K.C. Forman (New York: Oxford, 1998), 161–210; David C.

Lamberth, *William James and the Metaphysics of Experience* (Cambridge: Cambridge University Press, 1999). Proudfoot and Jantzen both acknowledge James's explanation of religious experience. Proudfoot sets it aside, however, because he views James as fundamentally uninterested in questions of origins (161–166). Jantzen dismisses it because it does not seek to explain the sorts of experiences that Christian mystics, considered historically, actually took to be central (296–300). Lamberth tends to downplay consciousness beyond the margin. Barnard recognizes the significance of consciousness beyond the margin for *Varieties* and discusses it at length (*Unseen Worlds*, 7, 170–179; "Origins," 182–188). His reading, while largely compatible with mine, is oriented toward philosophical discussions of mysticism, not theory and method in the study of religion.

10. David M. Wulff, *Psychology of Religion: Classic and Contemporary Approaches*, 2nd ed. (New York: Wiley, 1997), 28; emphasis added.

11. James, *Varieties*, 359–360, 402–405.

12. Henry S. Levinson, *The Religious Investigations of William James* (Chapel Hill: University of North Carolina Press, 1981), 116; John Smith, ed., *The Varieties of Religious Experience* in *The Works of William James* (Cambridge: Harvard University Press, 1985), 452; Robert Charles Powell, "The 'Subliminal' Versus the 'Subconscious,'" *Journal of the History of the Behavioral Sciences* 15 (1979): 156; Taylor, *William James on Consciousness Beyond the Margins*, 87; Barnard, *Unseen Worlds*, 173. Although all these scholars agree that James was referring to Myers, they are not agreed on the particular publication that marks this discovery. John Smith cites Myers, "Human Personality in the Light of Hypnotic Suggestion," in the *Proceedings of the Society for Psychical Research*; Powell cites Myers's long note appended to Gurney, Myers, and Podmore, *Phantasms of the Living* (1886); Levinson and Taylor do not cite any text. Barnard equates the discovery of "consciousness beyond the margin" with Myers's theory of the "subliminal self" and, following Jacques Barzun, *A Stroll with William James* (New York: Harper & Row, 1983), 229–230, claims James modestly attributed the idea of the subliminal self to Myers's 1892 essays when, in fact, James "had written an article on 'The Hidden Self,' using some hints from Janet and his own experimental observations" two years earlier (173).

13. The results of Janet's experiments were published serially in the *Revue Philosophique* between 1886 and 1889 and provided the basis for his thesis, *L'Automatisme Psychologique*, published in 1889. Pierre Janet's "Les actes inconscients et le dédoublement de la personnalité pendant le somnambulisme provoqué" appeared in the *Revue Philosophique* in 1886.

14. Alan Gauld, *A History of Hypnotism* (Cambridge: Cambridge University Press, 1992), 412. On Janet and the "subconscious," see: Pierre Janet, "A Symposium on the Subconscious," *Journal of Abnormal Psychology* 2 (1907): 58; Henri Ellenberger, *The Discovery of the Unconscious* (New York: Basic Books, 1970), 412*n*82; Frederick Myers, "The Subliminal Consciousness," *Proceedings of the Society for Psychical Research* 7 (1891–1892): 298–355; on Freud's concept of repression, see

68 ANN TAVES

Nathan Hale, *Freud and the Americans* (New York: Oxford University Press, 1995), 168–169 and *Repression and Dissociation: Implications for Personality Theory, Psychopathology, and Health,* ed. Jerome L. Singer (Chicago: University of Chicago Press, 1990).

15. Gauld, *Hypnotism,* 369–375; Janet writes: "We have insisted on these developments of a new psychological existence, no longer alternating with the normal existence of the subject, but absolutely simultaneous" (372–373). Gauld describes Léonie as a case of "three personalities coexisting as autonomous streams of consciousness, even though only one could be dominant at any given time" (378).

16. Sonu Shamdasani, "Automatic Writing and the Discovery of the Unconscious," *Journal of Archetypal Consciousness* 54 (Spring 1993): 111–118; J. P. Williams, "Psychical Research and Psychiatry in Late Victorian Britain: Trance as Ecstasy or Trance as Insanity," in *The Anatomy of Madness: Essays in the History of Psychiatry,* ed. W. Bynum, R. Porter, and M. Shephard, 3 vols. (London: Tavistock, 1985–1988), I:233–254. According to Shamdasani, "Williams focuses on the significance of the fact that Myers and his colleagues were putting forward the only alternative psychological and non-pathological view of trance states" (124*n*14).

17. As James explained in his *Principles of Psychology* (1890), theories of "unconscious cerebration" assumed the existence of unconscious mental states, i.e., mental states that were not conscious of themselves, to explain various "automatic" phenomena. James argued against the idea of unconscious mental states in *Principles,* suggesting two alternative explanations that he considered more plausible: "One is that the perceptions and volitions in habitual actions may be performed consciously, only so quickly and inattentively that no *memory* of them remains. Another is that the consciousness of these actions exists, but is *split-off* from the rest of the consciousness of the hemispheres." He noted that there were "numerous proofs of the reality of this split-off condition of portions of consciousness" that he planned to discuss later in the book (William James, *The Principles of Psychology* [New York: H. Holt, 1890], 167). It was the discovery of this evidence that James referred to in *Varieties* as "the most important step forward that has occurred in psychology since I have been a student" (190).

18. F. W. Myers, "Automatic Writing," *Proceedings of the Society for Psychical Research* 3 (1885): 24, 27; emphasis in original.

19. Hale, *Freud and the Americans,* 126–127; both Janet and Binet acknowledged their debt to Myers, see Shamdasani, "Automatic Writing," 118–119.

20. F. W. Myers, *Human Personality and Its Survival of Bodily Death,* ed. and abridged by L. H. Myers (London: Longmans, Green, 1907), 13. His statement of his basic position there reads:

The "conscious Self" of each of us, as we call it—the empirical, the supraliminal Self, as I should prefer to say,—does not comprise the whole of the consciousness or of the faculty within us. There exists a more comprehensive consciousness, a profounder faculty, which for the most part remains potential only so far as regards the life of earth, but from which the consciousness and the faculty of earth-life are mere selections, and which reasserts itself in its plentitude after the liberating change of death.

That "fourteen years since" is a reference to 1887 is suggested by the footnoted reference to Myers's article "Automatic Writing" (see note 18 above) and corroborated by an earlier statement that the publication of *Phantasms of the Living* in 1886 occurred fifteen years earlier (9).

21. James, *Principles*, 1213 (emphasis in original); see also 200–209, 1208 and "The Hidden Self," 373. In a review of French research, Myers referred to "the important point which M. Janet in France and Mr. Gurney in England have largely helped us to establish,—namely, the persistence of the hypnotic self, as a remembering and reasoning entity, during the reign of the primary self" (F. Myers, "French Experiments on Strata of Personality," *Proceedings of the Society for Psychical Research* 5 [1888–1889]: 377).

22. James, *Principles*, 1213.

23. Edmund Gurney, "Peculiarities of Certain Post-Hypnotic States," *Proceedings of the Society for Psychical Research* 4 (April 1887): 292–293.

24. In 1892, James wrote: "Gurney shares, therefore, with Janet and Binet, whose observations were made with widely differing subjects and methods, the credit of demonstrating the simultaneous existence of two different strata of consciousness, ignorant of each other, in the same person" (William James, *Essays in Psychical Research* [Cambridge: Harvard University Press, 1986], 95). "Gurney, Janet, Binet and others" are cited in a review essay in 1896 as "prov[ing]" that mutually disconnected currents of conscious life can simultaneously coexist in the same person" (William James, *Essays, Comments, and Reviews* [Cambridge: Harvard University Press, 1987], 527–529). In 1903, James states "that these other currents may not only alternate but may co-exist with each other is proved by Gurney's, Binet's, and Janet's discovery of Subjects who, receiving suggestions during hypnosis and forgetting them when wakened, nevertheless then wrote them out automatically and unconsciously as soon as a pencil was placed in their hands" (W. James, "Review of *Human Personality and its Survival of Bodily Death* by Frederic W. H. Myers," *Proceedings of the Society for Psychical Research* 18 [1903–1904]: 24). Alfred Binet, *Alterations of Personality* (New York: D. Appleton, 1896), 219–246, 325–343; Gauld, *Hypnotism*, 380–381.

25. James, *Varieties*, 190.

26. James, *Psychical Research*, 95; *The Will to Believe* (Cambridge: Harvard University Press, 1979), 230, emphasis added.

27. James, *Principles*, 1213. According to Hacking, Janet "formulated a theory of multiplicity, and its dynamics, a model suggested by his choice of French words such as *dissociation* and *désagrégation*. The word 'dissociation' entered English in 1890 thanks to William James, who was fascinated by French psychology, and who was deeply impressed by Janet as a person. Morton Prince . . . also

used the word in print in 1890, after his visit to France, and it was he who cemented it into English" (Hacking, *Rewriting the Soul,* 44).

28. Myers, "French Experiments," 387; Williams, "Psychical Research and Psychiatry," 242–243. Janet cites Gurney, "Stages of Hypnotic Memory" in "Les actes inconscients et la mémoire," *Revue philosophique* 24 (1888): 273.

29. Gauld, *Hypnotism,* 369–381, especially 379; Williams, "Psychical Research and Psychiatry," 234–235, 240. Janet, like Charcot, equated hysteria and hypnotism. Their views were challenged by the research of Liébeault and Bernheim of the Nancy school, who claimed that virtually all hypnotic phenomena up to and including somnambulism could be induced in mentally normal individuals (Gauld 327). Gauld gives extended treatment to the conflict between Charcot and his rivals at Nancy (297–362). F. W. H. Myers, his brother A. T. Myers, Edmund Gurney, and Morton Prince all visited Nancy (Gauld 336). In his discussion of hypnotic trance in the *Principles,* James attributes it not to animal magnetism nor "neurosis" (Charcot), but primarily to "suggestion" (Nancy), with the caveat that hypnosis did involve a change in the state of consciousness, i.e., "hypnotic trance" (Taylor, *Consciousness,* 38; Gauld, *Hypnotism,* 352; James, *Principles,* 1199–1201).

30. Frederic W. H. Myers, "The Subliminal Consciousness," *Proceedings of the Society for Psychical Research* 7 (1891–1892): 301.

31. In 1895, James wrote that when it came to theories of the mind, "no one . . . can be said to throw any more positive light than Mr. Myers or Janet" (James, *Essays, Comments and Reviews,* 529).

32. Shamdusani, "Automatic Writing," 111.

33. F. W. H. Myers, "Automatic Writing—III," *Proceedings of the Society for Psychical Research* 4 (1886–1887): 216.

34. Ibid. 239–240. Janet refers to Léonie as "L." in the article Myers is discussing. Myers writes that he will call her "Louise" rather than "L."

35. Ibid. 236–237, 245.

36. Ibid. 216.

37. Ibid. 254.

38. Ibid. 213.

39. Ibid.

40. James, *Varieties,* 15, 17, 26, 29.

41. Myers, "Automatic Writing—III," 254.

42. Ibid. 225.

43. Myers, "Automatic Writing—IV," *Proceedings of the Society for Psychical Research* 5 (1889): 522–523.

44. James, "The Hidden Self," 373; "What Psychical Research Has Accomplished," *Psychical Research,* 102, 98.

45. William James, "Frederic Myers's Service to Psychology" (1901), *Psychical Research,* 198; "Address of the President before the Society for Psychical Research" (1896), ibid. 132–133.

46. Myers, "Automatic Writing—IV," 522–524, emphasis added.

47. Ibid. 535, 538, 543.

48. Myers, "Subliminal Consciousness," 299–300; Gauld provides an extended discussion of Myers's idea of the subliminal consciousness, but does not root it firmly enough, in my view, in the research on secondary selves (Alan Gauld, *The Founders of Psychical Research* [London: Routledge & Kegan Paul, 1968], 275–299; *Hypnotism*, 393–400).

49. Myers, "Subliminal Consciousness," 301.

50. Ibid. 305.

51. Ibid. 313.

52. Ibid. 314, 325–326.

53. Ibid. 308–309.

54. Myers, "French Experiments," 389.

55. Proudfoot, *Religious Experience*, 162; "William James on an Unseen Order," *Harvard Theological Review* 93, 1 (2000): 51–66.

56. James, *Varieties,* 402.

57. Barnard misses this crucial point when he describes James as aligning "himself with the scientific authority and respectability of a psychological understanding of the subliminal origins of religious experiences, while simultaneously siding with the theological conviction that the 'higher power' that is contacted during salvific experiences is objective and external to the individual" (Barnard, "Origins," 187).

58. James, *Varieties,* 404, emphasis added.

59. Ibid. 381.

60. In his words, "the only novelty that I can imagine this course of lectures to possess lies in the breadth of the apperceiving mass," that is, "the mass of collateral phenomena, morbid or healthy, with which the various religious phenomena must be compared in order to understand them better" (ibid. 29).

61. Given the ambiguity of subconscious origins, James emphasized that all that emerged from (or through) the subconscious had to be tested in terms of "the way in which it works on the whole." This, James said, was his "empiricist criterion; and this criterion the stoutest insisters on supernatural origin have also been forced to use in the end" (ibid. 24–25).

62. David Lamberth has done a good job of reconstructing the metaphysical underpinnings of James's theory of religion; cf. "James's *Varieties* Reconsidered: Radical Empiricism, the Extra-Marginal, and Conversion," *American Journal of Theology and Philosophy* 15, 3 (1994): 257–267; *Metaphysics of Experience*, chapter 3.

63. William E. Paden, "Elements of a New Comparativism," in *A Magic Still Dwells*, ed. Kimberly C. Patton and Benjamin C. Ray (Berkeley: University of California Press, 2000), 187–188, 190.

64. William James, "Review of *Human Personality and Its Survival of Bodily Death*," 23. To quote James more fully, "The few [neurologists] who admit them [the 'evolutive,' 'superior,' or 'supernormal' phenomena" that interested Myers], are more likely to see in them another department of experience altogether than

to treat them as having continuous connection with the ordinary phenomena of mental dissociation." The situation has not changed dramatically since James wrote these words, although the current edition of the *Diagnostic and Statistical Manual of Mental Disorders* (or *DSM-IV*) is groping, rather haltingly, toward a less completely pathological understanding of dissociation.

65. The work of Grace Jantzen and Danièle Hervieu-Léger has been particularly helpful to me on this point. Cf. Jantzen, "Mysticism and Experience," 298–299; Jantzen, "A Mystical Core of Religion?," *Religious Studies* 26 (1990): 66, 69–71; Danièle Hervieu-Léger, *Religion as a Chain of Memory* (New Brunswick: Rutgers University Press, 2000).

66. William E. Arnal, "Definition," in *Guide to the Study of Religion*, ed. Willi Braun and Russell T. McCutcheon (London & New York: Cassell, 2000), 22.

67. Jonathan Z. Smith, *Drudgery Divine* (Chicago: University of Chicago Press, 1990), 52; F. J. P. Poole, "Metaphors and Maps: Towards Comparison in the Anthropology of Religion," *Journal of the American Academy of Religion* 54 (1986): 428.

68. Stewart E. Guthrie, "Projection," in *Guide to the Study of Religion*, ed. Willi Braun and Russell T. McCutcheon (London & New York: Cassell, 2000), 237; see also *Faces in the Clouds: A New Theory of Religion* (New York: Oxford, 1993), 41–61.

4

⚮

James's *Varieties* and the
"New" Constructivism

JEROME BRUNER

I

*I*t is puzzling, William James's impact on the human sciences in America, especially his impact on psychology. He is not much read anymore, nor has he been for three-quarters of a century—not, in any case, by psychologists, sociologists, and anthropologists. And *The Varieties of Religious Experience*, whose centenary we are celebrating, is rarely cited. Yet, for all that, William James has, without question, had a pervasive influence. But it has been an oblique and indirect influence—odd, given that psychology in America was virtually created by his magisterial *Principles of Psychology*. Indeed, it was his own Department of Philosophy that first made a place for aspiring psychology graduate students, and it continued to do so into the 1920s, when Psychology bolted in search of its own identity.

James has become a totemic figure, and as with all totemic figures, his influence is more atmospheric than substantive, more ideological than theoretical. His doctrine of pragmatism, for example, has been rendered into common sense, and technical interest in the doctrine has shifted from his writings to those of Charles Sanders Peirce, to pragmatism in epistemology rather than as an ethical guide. All this despite Richard Rorty's brilliant, decades-long effort to keep pragmatism in its broader perspective.[1] Ironically, there are probably more students in divinity schools than in psychology departments who read *The Varieties of Religious Experience*. But this is no more ironic than that the centenary of James's *Principles of Psychology* went virtually unnoticed in the psychological community a decade ago.

Perhaps the answer to this riddle is that James's pragmatic outlook has become so implicit in and so endemic to American thought that it is like the water in the famous proverb about the fish who will be the last to discover what he's been swimming in all along. James made pragmatism so self-evident that succeeding generations took it as their implicit starting point, and were lured thereafter into its less obvious implications—with one of which we shall be particularly concerned, "constructivism" or the "social construction of reality," as it is sometimes called. It was in *The Varieties of Religious Experience* that James had his first all-out constructivist fling, but it was no caprice. Rather, social constructivism, as I shall argue presently, is a natural if radical adjunct to James's pragmatism.

But before I turn to that matter, I want first to say a word about the indirect, the oblique impact of the Jamesian legacy on my own generation, for we were the generation that launched the Cognitive Revolution once we grew up. It was no accident that the first skirmishes in that revolution took place in a building called William James Hall, a block or two from the Harvard Yard. Those skirmishes were nourished by the Jamesian spirit, and while they were principally empirical rather than philosophical, they laid the groundwork, I believe, for what later came to be "the constructivist point of view." There were visiting philosophers in William James Hall—like Nelson Goodman—but they were there for a year, invited to share with the resident psychologists, sociologists, and anthropologists the task of redefining the study of man. William James was ever present, obliquely, in the background, *res ipse loquitur*, as lawyers like to put it.

Let me back up in time. Harvard Psychology, when I arrived as a young graduate student just before World War II, shared Emerson Hall in the Harvard Yard with Philosophy, which occupied the first two floors; Psychology had the top two. The elegant stairway to the second floor, with its panoramic window overlooking the yard, was the principal locus of contact between the two disciplines, along with the Robbins Library of Philosophy and Psychology, just at the head of that flight of stairs. Graduate students from the two departments mixed little, not even in Robbins, where the rule of silence reinforced natural indifference. Even the young "lefties" in the two departments, who knew one another from demonstrations, shared politics rather than scholarship.

How did I land at Harvard? The revered image of William James surely lured me—but there the story takes an odd twist. My senior adviser at Duke, where I'd been an undergraduate, was the formidable Englishman, William McDougall, F.R.S. When I told him I was leaning toward Harvard for graduate study, he frowned: "So antimentalist, Bruner, I fled the place." With William James still in mind, I went anyway.

But fortunately, McDougall had missed something, something pragmatic and most typically Harvard of those days. For Harvard under James Bryant Conant was still wedded to letting opposing points of view battle it out, letting the judgment of the world decide. So Harvard Psychology, though centered on positivist sensation-perception-psychophysics, also gave room to some dedicated antipositivist mentalists—the most outspoken being Gordon Allport, a scholar of deep convictions. Allport, interestingly and perhaps typically, was, I would say, an undeclared Jamesian. It was he who carried the Jamesian flag, although nobody ever labeled it that way. James was "history."

Allport's most passionate doctrine was what came to be called the functional autonomy of motives, which he invoked principally against Freud's historicist emphasis on the child being father to the man. The functional autonomy of motives argues that habits themselves become their own motives once established in a way of life. It is a doctrine, as some of you will recognize, right out of chapter 4 of James's *Principles*, the one on "Habit"—the fisherman keeps going to sea despite the dangers, the discomforts, the disappointments, an established habit with its own motive and with a version of reality constructed to support it. We shall meet it again as central to the argument of *The Varieties of Religious Experience.*

The debate over functional autonomy was, of course, my Harvard generation's subliminal induction into Jamesian thought. Note, though, that *The Varieties of Religious Experience* was never assigned to us as class reading—though most of us had spent some rich hours with it by the time we were done, more as *samizdat* than assigned reading. Something about it got to us, and helped form a young generation's unconscious.

II

Now to return to *Varieties* and its crypto-radical constructivism. Constructivism is the view, of course, that "reality" is made, not found—the fisherman's world in that chapter on habits in *Principles* is of the fisherman's making. Constructivism even finds its way into so unlikely a chapter of *Varieties* as "The Value of Saintliness." James is discussing the ever-changing nature of religious beliefs, noting particularly the shift from religious ritual and sacrifice to more "inward" doctrines.

> Today a deity who should require bleeding sacrifices to placate him would be too sanguinary to be taken seriously. Even if powerful historical credentials were put forward in his favor, we would not look at them. Once, on the contrary, his cruel appetites were of themselves credentials. They positively recommended him to men's imaginations in ages when such coarse signs of power were respected and no others could be understood. Such deities then were worshipped because such fruits were relished. . . . So soon as the fruits began to seem quite worthless; so soon as they conflicted with indispensable human ideals . . . ; so soon as they appeared childish, contemptible, or immoral when reflected on, the deity grew discredited and was erelong neglected and forgotten.[2]

Indeed, religious doctrines even change in ways that run counter to the ideals of their originators, a point James illustrates with a gentle dig at his Bostonian townsmen:

> Luther, says Emerson, would have cut off his right hand rather than nail his theses to the door at Wittenberg, if he had supposed that they were destined to lead to the pale negations of Boston Unitarianism.[3]

And then he brings his discussion to a rousing pragmatic conclusion: "The gods we stand by are the gods we need and can use, the gods whose demands on us are reinforcements of our demands on ourselves and on one another."[4] Be not confused, he argues: "No religion has ever yet owed its prevalence to 'apodictic certainty.'"[5]

There are moments, indeed, when James even sounds like our present-day arch-constructivist, Michel Foucault.[6]

> The monarchical type of sovereignty was, for example, so ineradicably planted in the mind of our forefathers that a dose of cruelty and arbitrariness in their deity seems positively to have been required by their imagination. They called the cruelty "retributive justice" and a God without it would certainly have struck them as not "sovereign" enough.[7]

So there we have William James, in 1902, already a constructivist, already committed to a perspectival view of religious experience, of all experience. And, indeed, religious experience in the Jamesian account not only is personal but reflects the cultural conditions in which it is born. Thus does absolute monarchy breed a taste for an absolute sovereign God!

James tries to make it clear right from that oddly titled opening chapter, "Religion and Neurology," that religious experience is like *all* experience, constructed like all human experience is constructed. At which point he begins his case in earnest:

> I am neither a theologian, nor a scholar learned in the history of religions, nor an anthropologist. Psychology is the only branch of knowledge in which I am particularly versed. To the psychologist the religious propensities of man must be at least as interesting as any other of the facts pertaining to his mental constitution. . . . The natural thing for me would be to invite you to a descriptive survey of those religious propensities. . . . [8]

But he assures his readers forthwith that his is not the way of reductivism: let religious experience be taken *as* experienced and, indeed, at its most fully realized.

> I must confine myself to those more developed subjective phenomena recorded in literature produced by articulate and fully self-conscious men, in works of piety and autobiography. . . . The documents that will most concern us will be those of the men who were most accomplished in the religious life and best able to give an intelligible account of their ideas and motives.[9]

Therefore, study the most religious man at his most religious moment—do so *existentially* rather than *spiritually*. Let us inquire: "What is the nature of [religious experience]? how does it come about? what is its constitution, origin, and history?" Our task is not with its spiritual side, "What is its importance, meaning, or significance, now that it is once here?" And then, "Neither [the existential nor the spiritual] . . . can be deduced from the other. They proceed from diverse preoccupations."[10] Therefore, let not the devout take offense: the existential approach is not intended as a "degradation . . . deliberately seeking to discredit the religious side of life." What if religious geniuses show "all sorts of peculiarities which are ordinarily classed as pathological"? It is the products of their genius, the realities they construct that must concern us, proof of which he finds, recall, even in that bizarre extract from George Fox's diary where he has been instructed by God to enter Lichfield crying, "Wo to the bloody city of Lichfield!" And though Fox, in James's words, "was a psychopath or détraqué of the deepest dye," everybody from Oliver Cromwell down to the local magistrate "acknowledged his superior powers." Rather than "ignore these pathological aspects of the subject. We must describe and name them just as they occurred in non-religious men." Their spiritual value is not undone "if lowly origin be asserted."[11]

III

Consider James in this existential mode. His decorum is that of today's "psychological anthropologist" or "cultural psychologist," bent on describing situated realities in cultural context—reminiscent, indeed, of a Clifford Geertz trying to interpret the rationale of the Javanese cockfight, or of a Victor Turner in search of the meaning of Ndembu rituals, or of an E. E. Evans-Pritchard painstakingly unraveling the mystery of chicken poisoning as a divine juridical procedure among the Azande.[12] Like them, James is in pursuit of the compelling realities experienced by religious men in their religious moments. Like them, he asks what kinds of reality they construct and how their constructions serve them and serve their communities.

But he does not stop there. For James is also profoundly interested in *how* people construct their realities—interested as a psychologist whose lifelong preoccupation had been with the vagaries of *consciousness*. In his conception, mind is composed of "fields of consciousness," each with a center of attention of its own, each seeking to preempt the whole of experience. The realities we finally experience are, then, outcomes of the inner battle for the focus of consciousness. Not surprising, then, that the second half of *Varieties* is given over to the inner maneuvers by which fields of consciousness gain control over experience, the melodramas of religious consciousness—conversion, prayer, the employment of beauty, confession, and the rest.

Typical is James's account of the "religion of healthy-mindedness," the happy plight of the "once-born."

> . . . we must admit that any persistent enjoyment may produce the sort of religion which consists in a grateful admiration of the gift of so happy an existence. . . . It is perhaps not surprising that men come to regard the happiness which a religious belief affords as a proof of its truth.[13]

Unsatisfied with that simplicity, he turns to a more subtle view, one expressed by the less famous younger brother of the famous Cardinal Newman—the classicist Francis William Newman:

> "God has two families of children on this earth," says Francis W. Newman, "*the once-born and the twice-born,*" and the once-born he describes as follows: "They see God not as a strict Judge nor as a Glorious Potentate; but as the animating Spirit of a beautiful harmonious world, Beneficent and Kind, Merciful as well as Pure. . . . They do not look back into themselves. Hence they are not distressed by their own imperfections. . . . "[14]

But James, though at one with Newman about these two basic "temperaments," is not prepared to see them placed separately in two kinds of "children of God." Rather, he sees them at odds with each other inside each of us, negating each other: "When happiness is actually in possession, the thought of evil can no more acquire the feeling of reality than the thought of good can gain reality when melancholy rules."[15] And he goes on: "Since you make them evil or good by your own thoughts about them, it is the ruling of your thoughts which proves to be your principal concern."[16] But not the ruling of your thoughts alone, for the culture also provides opportunities, almost genres for constructing our religious experiences. And he illustrates from his own contemporary world:

> The advance of liberalism, so-called, in Christianity, during the past fifty years, may fairly be called a victory of healthy-mindedness within the church over the morbidness with which the old hell-fire theology was more harmoniously related.[17]

Indeed, James goes so far as to characterize genres of the twice-born, "the world-sick soul," and even singles out classic Stoicism and Epicureanism as examples:

> The Epicurean said: "Seek not to be happy, but rather to escape un-happiness; strong happiness is always linked with pain; therefore hug the shore." The Stoic said, "The only genuine good that life can yield a man is the free possession of his own soul; all other goods are lies." Each of these philosophies is in its degree a philosophy of de-spair in nature's boons. Trustful abandonment to the joys that freely offer has entirely departed from both Epicurean and Stoic.[18]

These are the kinds of belief that "mark the conclusion of what we call the once-born period," and then souls "leave the world in the shape of an un-reconciled contradiction, and seek no higher unity."[19]

So life, then, is a battleground of once-born joys and twice-born de-spairs, and the search is on for a religious reality that can accommodate both. How well James knew this struggle, he who had suffered disabling bouts of depression! Might that have accounted for his seeing the twice-born as a "sick" soul, with conversion as an escape from dark despair into light and affirmation?

Some have commented that James's view of *religious* experience (par-ticularly of its "healthy-minded" version) was too Protestant by twice—or even too *New England* Protestant in Perry Miller's sense.[20] Surely it is odd to pin the label of "sick-minded" on Epicureanism and Stoicism. Is Catholicism also "sick-minded," weighted as it is with Original Sin? I can understand why some critics (even one of the participants in our sympo-sium) see *The Varieties of Religious Experience* as an apologia, even a "plug" for Protestantism. And surely there are some shockingly blatant parochialisms in the book, for William James, for all his genius, never fully rose above his background.

But even with his parochialism showing, James still has some arresting things to say about the battle for consciousness in religious experience, particularly in conversion, but even in the mundane practice of prayer. Let me return briefly to his theory of consciousness to make the matter clearer.

For James, as for Freud and even Helmholtz before that, there is not only consciousness in the ordinary sense of full awareness but also a world of subliminal consciousness. The achievement of full awareness, as we've already seen, comes with the conquest by some "fields of consciousness" over others. Let me quote from a revealing footnote in his chapter on conversion:

> The subliminal region, whatever else it may be, is . . . for the accumulation of vestiges of sensible experience (whether attentively or inattentively registered) and for their elaboration according to ordinary psychological or logical laws into results that end by attaining such a "tension" that they may at times enter consciousness. . . . It thus is "scientific" to interpret all otherwise unaccountable invasive alterations of consciousness as results of the tension of subliminal memories reaching the bursting point.[21]

Achieved experience, religious or not, is then the outcome of a struggle between familiar everyday awareness and subliminally active conceptions of the possible, the forbidden, the less familiar. James gracefully admits that this struggle was poorly understood by the psychology of his day—and it is not much better understood today, despite Freud and a century of research since those Gifford Lectures. But what *is* plain today is that the "realities" we construct are indeed the final outcomes of a "competition" for center-stage awareness. In that sense, James was indeed prescient. And his intuitions about the weapons used in that battle for consciousness (even when he is being Protestant parochial) are still interesting. I want to consider three of them briefly—the employment of the aesthetic in religious experience, the significance of confession, and the uses of prayer.

The aesthetic first:

> I promised to say nothing of ecclesiastical systems in these lectures.
> I may be allowed, however, to put in a word at this point on the way

in which their satisfaction of certain aesthetic needs contributes to their hold on human nature.[22]

Whereupon he offers this bit of stunningly Protestant sentiment:

> To an imagination used to the perspectives of dignity and glory [as in the High Church], the naked gospel scheme seems to offer an almshouse for a palace. . . . It pauperizes the monarchical imagination![23]

And then,

> The strength of these aesthetic sentiments makes it rigorously impossible, it seems to me, that Protestantism, however superior in profundity it may be to Catholicism, should at the present day succeed in making many converts from the more venerable ecclesiasticism.[24]

He may, of course be dead wrong—witness the rise of scrubbed-down fundamentalism—yet the conjecture is interesting, rather reminiscent of Henry Adams's famous "All the steam in the world could not, like the Virgin, build Chartres." The place of the aesthetic in religious experience is still an unwritten chapter.

When it comes to confession, James reverts to a strikingly functionalist view: "For him who confesses, shams are over and realities have begun; he has exteriorized his rottenness. If he has not actually got rid of it . . . he lives at least upon a basis of veracity."[25] And this time he is mindful of the details of different religious cultures—inquiring, for example, whether the one-on-one ritual confession of Catholicism reflects a different worldview from that of the Protestant. As he puts it,

> The Catholic church, for obvious utilitarian reasons, has substituted auricular confession to one priest for the more radical act of public confession. We English-speaking Protestants, in the general self-reliance and unsociability of our nature, seem to find it enough if we take God alone into our confidence.[26]

I must admit that the cultural psychologist in me immediately thought to consult the famous Yale Cross-Cultural Index. Is there a heading for "Confession" in its copious collection? What do we know about the forms of confession in the cultures of the world and how these affect and are affected by worldviews?

But perhaps it is on the topic of prayer that James's pragmatic functionalism comes to full expression: "Prayer is religion in act."

> Religion is nothing if it be not the vital act by which the entire mind seeks to save itself by clinging to the principle from which it draws life. This act of prayer . . . [puts one's being] in a personal relation . . . with the mysterious power of which it feels the presence. . . . The conviction that something is genuinely transacted in this consciousness is the very core of living religion.[27]

For James, of course, prayer includes the myriad means by which we make our *personal* appeal to unknown powers. It represents, as it were, our means of seeking higher support for our constructed version of reality.

It is not so much that James "gets it right" about the place of aesthetics, confession, and prayer in religious experience, but rather that he feels impelled to find their role in shaping such experience. He is in pursuit of *how* religious realities are constructed, and considers that task to be the heart of his mission—to search for the *means whereby religious experience is created.*

IV

Let me conclude, then, with a few comments about the subtle place of *The Varieties of Religious Experience* not only in shaping modern, postbehaviorist psychology but also in nurturing contemporary sensibility. His impact, as I've said, has been atmospheric rather than direct and textual. What he was proposing was a rich descriptive science of man based on "thick description" of human experience, to use Clifford Geertz's term. "Thick description," to be sure, was in the spirit of James's times, but it was literary rather than scientific—witness Nathaniel Hawthorne and Herman Melville, whom he had read, and Edith Wharton, who later read him. His ultimate aim in *Varieties* was, however, to explicate "thick description" through a science of psychology adequate to the task, to do so with full respect and without reductivism.

Why did he choose religious experience as his central topic? Why not family experience, business experience, or whatever? He never quite tells us. He might, of course, have been trying to make sense of the bizarre religious beliefs of his gifted and eccentric Swedenborgian father. Perhaps. My own guess is that he chose it because it permitted him to explore human reality making without having to venture into the constraining ontology of the "real" world of rocks and molecules, nerve fibers and brain centers. He, New England Protestant, was in search of the *psychological* constraints on "world building" just as, a decade or so later, Emile Durkheim, a French Jew, set out to explore its sociological functions and constraints.[28]

James would have welcomed Durkheim, much as he would have welcomed those three distinguished modern anthropologists earlier mentioned who, more than a half century after *Varieties*, tried to follow a Jamesian path in understanding the intricate beliefs and practices of the preliterate Balinese, Ndembu, and Azande. It is a tribute to William James that today, a century after it appeared, *The Varieties of Religious Experience* stands grandly as ever, not as a quaint century-old precursor from the past but as a beginning of the present-in-the-making, the genuine article. Not surprising that it continues to lure us.

NOTES

1. Richard Rorty, *Consequences of Pragmatism: Essays, 1972–1980* (Minneapolis: University of Minnesota Press, 1982).

2. William James, *The Varieties of Religious Experience* (Cambridge: Harvard University Press, 1985), 264. All page references are to this edition.

3. Ibid. 265.

4. Ibid. 324.

5. Ibid. 266.

6. See particularly Michel Foucault, *Discipline and Punish: The Birth of the Prison*, tr. Alan Sheridan (New York: Vintage, 1979).

7. James, *Varieties*, 265.

8. Ibid. 12.

9. Ibid.

10. Ibid. 13.

11. Ibid. 16–17.

12. See Clifford Geertz, *The Interpretation of Cultures* (New York: Basic Books, 1973); Victor W. Turner, *The Drums of Affliction: A Study of Religious Processes Among the Ndembu of Zambia* (Oxford: Clarendon Press, 1968); and E. E. Evans-Pritchard, *Witchcraft, Oracles and Magic Among the Azande* (Oxford: Clarendon

Press, 1937). It is worth noting that all three of these classics appeared long after *The Varieties of Religious Experience*, and that none of them refers to that book—*sic transit gloria mundi!*

13. James, *Varieties*, 71.

14. James, *Varieties*, 73, quoting Francis William Newman, *The Soul: Its Sorrows and its Aspirations*, 3rd ed. (1852), 89, 81. A more accessible work dealing with these issues more personally is Newman's *Phases of Faith* (New York: Humanities Press, 1970).

15. James, *Varieties*, 87.

16. Ibid.

17. Ibid. 81.

18. Ibid. 121.

19. Ibid. 121–122.

20. Perry Miller, *The New England Mind: The Seventeenth Century* (Cambridge: Harvard University Press, 1954).

21. James, *Varieties*, 192*n*4.

22. Ibid. 362.

23. Ibid. 363.

24. Ibid.

25. Ibid. 364.

26. Ibid. 365.

27. Ibid. 366.

28. Emile Durkheim, *The Elementary Forms of Religious Life*, tr. Karen Fields (New York: Free Press, 1995).

5

∞

Some Inconsistencies in
James's *Varieties*

RICHARD RORTY

*I*n *The Varieties of Religious Experience* William James asks
some good questions, but he does not offer a coherent set
of answers to them. The book is riddled with inconsistencies.
These are not merely incidental. They stem from James's inability to make up his mind between arguing that supernaturalism might be true because it might be good for you and arguing that it is in fact true because there is ample experiential
evidence for it. The most prominent among the inconsistencies I have in mind are the clashing definitions he offers of the
term "religious" and the differing meanings of the term "experience" that he tacitly invokes.

The ambiguities in James's use of the term "religion" appear when we press such questions as: Does any example of
what he calls a "total reaction upon life" (36) by a human being
count as a religion?[1] Or can one fruitfully distinguish a religious reaction from a merely moral one, and distinguish both
from Nietzsche's, whose reaction James describes as "merely
peevish"? Can one be religious even if one repudiates all forms

of supernaturalism, even the fuzzy Arnoldian idea of a power not our-selves that makes for righteousness and the equally fuzzy Emersonian idea that "the universe has a divine soul of order, which soul is moral, being also the soul within the soul of man" (35)? Would it still count as being religious if one regarded this divine soul as, to use James's words, "a mere quality like the eye's brilliancy or the skin's softness" rather than as "a self-conscious life like the eye's seeing or the skin's feeling" (35)?

The ambiguities in his use of the term "experience" appear when we try to pin down James's answers to the following questions: Are the caus-es of religious experience entirely irrelevant to their value for human life, or do we have empirical evidence that these experiences have a supernat-ural cause, and therefore reason to believe in the existence of an entity unknown to natural science? More generally, are experiences the sorts of things that come with tracers indicating their origin, or is the question of origin left entirely up for grabs by the intrinsic nature of an experience? Does the experience itself dictate the language in which it is described or is it, like the beetle in the box described by Wittgenstein, entirely irrele-vant to the linguistic clothing that the experiencer drapes about it?

One selection of passages from *Varieties* gives a set of answers to these latter questions that would justify reading the book as a work of natural theology. These passages suggest that we should treat James as an empir-ical inquirer who, after having studied a range of human experiences, is in a position to conclude that we have as good evidence for the existence of "a wider self from which saving experiences come"—a self-conscious nonhuman life—as we do for the existence of penguins. On this reading, experience makes an end run around physical science and leads us straight to the sort of being for whose existence Clifford thought there to be insufficient evidence.

Another selection of passages, however, leads to a reading of James as wholly indifferent to the question of the existence of God. On this reading, James is interested only in how human beings manage to get through life without being overwhelmed by despair (or, as we call it nowadays, de-pression). This second set of passages suggests that we can reduce what James calls the "wider self through which saving experiences come" (405) either to the believer's own subconscious self, which Freud said was suf-fused with infantile fantasies, or to what Dewey, in *A Common Faith*, called "the community of causes and consequences in which we, together with those not born, are enmeshed." This is the community Dewey went on to describe as "the widest and deepest symbol of the mysterious totality of being the imagination calls the universe."[2]

Either a Freudian or a Deweyan understanding of this wider self is entirely compatible with a belief that James professed to find intolerable: that we humans are like a tribe encamped upon the surface of a frozen lake, waiting for the inevitable melting, the moment when the universe will no longer contain any traces of our joys and sorrows. Freud and Dewey were, like Clifford, able to accept the second law of thermodynamics with an equanimity that James found impossible.

To make James a natural theologian, engaged in accumulating empirical evidence with a view to satisfying skeptics like Clifford that they have missed something, we have to focus on the sort of passage that occurs in abundance toward the end of the chapter called "Conclusions." Here James says that "Religion, in her fullest exercise of function, is not a mere illuminator of facts already elsewhere given, not a mere passion, like love, which views things in a rosier light . . . it is something more, namely, a postulator of new *facts*." Religious experiences, on this account, support the view that the world has "a natural constitution different at some points from that which a materialistic world would have" (407–408).

James calls this view an "over-belief," but he is never sure whether it is simply the sort of belief to which one has a right, even without evidence of a sort that Clifford needs to take seriously, or whether it is a belief for which the accumulated testimonies that fill the pages of *Varieties* provide evidence that Clifford has a duty to take into account. But most of the last chapter takes the latter tack. At its very end James confronts Clifford directly and by name, calls his view "humbug," and says that "the total expression of human experience, as I view it objectively, invincibly urges me beyond the narrow 'scientific' bounds. Assuredly, the real world is of a different temperament—more intricately built than physical science allows" (408). But this triumphant announcement of invincibility is hard to reconcile with James's cautionary remarks, earlier in the same chapter. There he says: "the most I can do is . . . to offer something that may fit the facts so easily that your scientific logic will find no plausible pretext for vetoing your impulse to welcome it as true" (402).

This more cautious stance is the one James had adopted in "The Will to Believe." In that essay he had been content to say simply that the religious have as much right to their outlook as Clifford does to his. Establishing this right can be read as one of the principal motives for developing the pragmatic view of truth and knowledge that James had outlined in his 1898 lecture "Philosophical Conceptions and Practical Results" and that he would, after completing *Varieties*, expound in detail in *Pragmatism*.

I read the latter book as saying: we can get some useful practical results out of science, and other useful practical results out of religion, so there is no reason not to have both; conflict arises only if we ask a bad question, namely, which of the two corresponds to the way the world really is? But the "Conclusions" chapter of *Varieties* cannot be read as saying this. Instead it says: religion tells you more than science does about what the world really is, but since this "more" will never get in science's way, your "scientific logic" should not object to it.

In what I have written about James in the past I have emphasized the similarities between his and Nietzsche's debunkings of the traditional idea that we have a duty to bring our views into correspondence with reality. I have focused on the willingness of both philosophers to say that the utility of a belief is the only judge of its truth. If James had pursued this line of thought consistently, he would have said that Nietzsche's outlook, peevish though it might seem, was the one Nietzsche had found most useful. It was the one that gave him the courage and energy to write his books and, as Nehamas has put it, to live life as literature. The delight Nietzsche took in the thought of eternal recurrence, and in getting rid of one God surrogate after another, James might have said, played the same role in Nietzsche's life that the sense of the presence of God played in the lives of saints and mystics. This was the same role that the conviction that natural science was the be-all and end-all played in Clifford's life, and that the belief that natural science was *not* the whole story played in Henry James Senior's life. Had James carried through on his pragmatism, he would have simply let "religious" be a synonym for "vitally important to a person's self-image" and let it go at that. He would not have tried to discriminate between "total reactions upon life" that are religious and those that are not. He would have called Nietzsche's total reaction as religious as Arnold's or Emerson's.

Had James consistently taken this route, he would not have raised the question of whether "the personal religion of which I propose to treat" does or does not "contain some elements which morality pure and simple does not" (33). He would have carried through on the thought that "religious awe is the same organic thrill which we feel in a forest in twilight" (31). He would have said not only that "the Stoic, Buddhist and Christian saints" share the same feelings and the same conduct (397) but that many defiantly atheistic moralists do as well. This would have led him to say what Dewey later did say:

> Those who hold to the notion that there is a definite kind of experience that is itself religious, by that very fact make out of it something specific, as a kind of experience that is marked off from experience as aesthetic, scientific, moral, political; from experience as companionship and friendship. But "religious" as a quality of experience signifies something that may belong to all these experiences. It is the polar opposite of some type of experience that can exist by itself.[3]

Dewey went on to conclude that all that a report of a religious experience can be said to "prove" is "the existence of some complex of conditions that have operated to effect an adjustment in life, an orientation, that brings with it a sense of security and peace."[4] Reinforcing the point, Dewey said: "It is the claim of religions that they effect this generic and enduring change in attitude. I should like to turn the statement around and say that whenever this change takes place there is a definitely religious attitude."[5]

This Deweyan line of thought would have been a natural one for the author of "Philosophical Conceptions and Practical Results" to have pursued, but it is not the most salient line of thought in *Varieties*. It comes to the surface of the text only by fits and starts. Consider, for example, James's italicized definition of "religion" in the second chapter: "the feelings, acts and experiences of individual men in their solitude, so far as they apprehend themselves to stand in relation to whatever they may consider the divine." When pressed about what counts as being considered divine, James is sometimes inclined to anticipate Tillich by saying that anything counts as divine that is a symbol of ultimate concern. Such genial tolerance can, for example, be read into his assertion that "The divine can mean no single quality, it must mean a group of qualities, by being champions of which in alternation, different men may all find worthy missions" (384). But passages such as that one are contradicted by those in which he defines "the religious life" in such a way as to ensure that no committed naturalist can lead it (see, for example, 382).

The pragmatic reduction of experiences to their effect on practice is prominent in the first chapter of *Varieties,* but by the last chapter it has been displaced. In the first chapter, "Religion and Neurology," James is concerned to brush aside the claim of "medical materialism" that many religious experiences are symptoms of mental pathology. "When we think certain states of mind superior to others," James asks, "is it ever because of what we know concerning their organic antecedents? No! it is always for two entirely different reasons. It is either because we take an immediate delight in them; or else it is because we believe them to bring us good consequential fruits for life" (21). Had he stuck to this line of thought, he would have said that it hardly matters whether the sense of a wider self from which saving experiences come is caused by a chance surplus of serotonin or, as the last chapter of the book holds, by an immaterial entity that is itself the remote efficient cause of a rearrangement of neural impulses. *All* that matters is the consequential fruits for life of that sense, so the question of which "total reactions to life" are religious can be set aside.

The purely pragmatic view, the one characteristic of the early chapters of *Varieties,* would urge that only short-term or long-term happiness matters when judging the worth of either a short-term experience or a long-term outlook. That methodological principle may seem to lie behind James's claim, in the chapter on "The sick soul," that "the purely naturalistic look at life, however enthusiastically it may begin, is sure to end in sadness" (119). But of course that assertion amounts to the very dubious empirical claim that naturalists like Clifford are incapable of the happiness achieved by Wesley and Emerson. In such passages, James simply turns a blind eye to all the joyful naturalists—people like Marx, Nietzsche, and Dewey, who are as eschatologically exuberant as any Christian, but whose descriptions of the universe are naturalistic through and through.

To sum up: James is torn between a Deweyan redefinition of "religious," to which pragmatism would seem naturally to lead, and the desire to confine the term "religious" to something that covers Arnold and Emerson but not Nietzsche or Marx. He is also torn between saying that we should adopt Arnold's and Emerson's quasi-theism because naturalism leads to despair and saying that we should do so on the basis of evidential experience. He dithers between saying that quasi-theism is good for you and saying that therapeutic efficacy is not the only thing Arnold and Emerson have going for them. This latter tension is between pragmatism and empiricism—not empiricism in the sense of Bacon's claim that one should base scientific conclusions on observational results, but in the sense that an experience might, all by itself, give one reason to change one's outlook on the world—to shift, for example, from naturalism to some form of supernaturalism.[6]

The tension I have been describing can be exhibited in more detail by turning to the second set of ambiguities I distinguished earlier—ambiguities in the meaning of the term "experience." These appear as soon as one asks whether James subscribes to what Wilfrid Sellars called "the myth of the Given," which Wittgenstein helped us dissolve in his discussion of private sensations and private beetles in *Philosophical Investigations*. In Sellars's and Wittgenstein's view, there is no such thing as the intrinsic content of an experience. To report an experience is simply to respond to being in a certain brain state with whatever sentences one's linguistic community has programmed one to use in that situation. If this view is right, then a change from a religious to a nonreligious outlook, or vice versa, can never be a matter of drawing information from the content of a new experience. The desirability of such a change can be evaluated only by reference to the practical advantages of switching from one linguistic community to another—for example, from responding to certain brain states with Freudian sentences rather than Christian ones, or vice versa. Only if Wittgenstein and Sellars are wrong can "I abandoned naturalism because of an experience of God that I had" be an acceptable explanation of someone's conversion.

In Sellars's view, there is no *tertium quid* called "experiential content" that intervenes between the altered state of the nervous system and the verbal behavior that ensues upon that alteration. The existence of such an intermediary is the issue that, in contemporary philosophical debates, sets Brandom against McDowell and Dennett against Chalmers. Sometimes, especially in chapter 1, James uses "experience" in the merely Sellarsian sense of "introspectively reportable change in the nervous system, whether externally or internally caused, that produces changes in belief." But most of the time he uses it in the bad old Lockean way—as a name for entities strutting their stuff on the stage of the Cartesian inner theater, entities that can be studied closely in order to determine what description fits them best.

The Sellars-Wittgenstein-Brandom-Dennett view is obviously congenial to pragmatism. For it reduces the experience of seeing something red, or of the presence of God, to the behavior that is induced by that experience. It asks about the effect on conduct of such experiences rather than the intrinsic, phenomenological character of the experiences themselves. It thinks of "experiential content" of a belief not as something that may or may not correspond to something real but rather as consisting entirely in the inferences that a particular linguistic community permits to be drawn from and to it.

A Sellarsian would never say, for example, what James says in order to fend off Freud, namely that if one looks at "the immediate content of the religious experience" one will see "how wholly disconnected it is from the content of the sexual consciousness" (19n). That strikes Sellarsians as just as bad as saying that pains certainly don't feel like brain processes, or that introspection will reveal whether one is truly in love or merely inflamed by passion. Sellarsians can see many reasons to agree or disagree with Freud's account of the origins of religious beliefs, but none of these reasons is the result of phenomenological inquiry.

Another way to put the contrast between the Sellarsian and the traditional empiricist view is to say that for a pragmatist like Dewey, whose views are untrammeled by any form of empiricist foundationalism, it is misleading to say, as James does, that "religious experience . . . spontaneously and inevitably engenders myths, superstitions, dogmas, creeds and metaphysical theologies" (342). This is no more accurate than it would be to say that sensory experience spontaneously and inevitably generates cosmological hypotheses, or that moral experience spontaneously and inevitably generates legal codes. The creeds, the hypotheses, and the codes are all generated by the attempts of human individuals and communities to solve their problems, to lead happier lives. "The immediate content of experience" is a wheel that plays no part in the mechanisms that produce solutions to such problems. Appeal to such content is always an empty, "dormitive power" explanation.

James was—unfortunately in my view—a radical empiricist as well as a pragmatist. His version of empiricism is nicely summed up in the reason he gives for thinking it false that religion is an outdated survival mechanism, an obsolete way of solving problems that can now be solved without it. He thinks that view shallow, he says, because "as soon as we deal with private and personal phenomena as such, we deal with realities in the completest sense of the term" (393). This is the view that he shared with Bergson, and that led him to adumbrate such notions as "a world of pure experience." But to a Sellarsian, the idea of such a world is a chimera, just as are "the phenomenological attitude" and "the first-person point of view."

It is one thing to say that one's private hopes, fears, and fantasies have rights that trump Clifford's claim that nobody has a right to believe anything unsupported by evidence. Granting such rights is the point both of "The Will to Believe" essay and of the passage I quoted earlier about the need for human diversity, which urges that "different men may all find worthy missions." It is also the point of a passage that James quotes from Leuba in his "Conclusions'" chapter (399), in which Leuba says that the question of whether God exists is irrelevant to the religious life, as long as belief in him is useful to the believer. It is quite another thing, however, to set up a metaphysics of feeling in opposition to the metaphysics of cognition common to Hegel, Green, and Royce. Pragmatism, when disconnected from empiricism, has no metaphysics—no views about what is real "in the completest sense of the term."

Both "The Will to Believe" and the passage James cites from Leuba are quite clear that our feelings have a right, in certain cases, to dictate our beliefs. Both are equally clear that in such matters there is no residual question of the form "But are those beliefs objectively true?" Yet in "Conclusions" James takes the latter question seriously and fudges the issue. He does so most blatantly when he says that "That unshareable feeling which each one of us has of the pinch of his individual destiny may be disparaged for its egotism, may be sneered at as unscientific, but it is the one thing that fills up the measure of our concrete actuality, and any would-be existent that should lack such a feeling, or its analogue, would be a piece of reality only half made up" (393–394).

This sentence runs together the question "What is important for a human life?" with the question "What exists?" Both Leuba and "The Will to Believe" essay had been careful to keep these questions apart. The same fudging is found a page later when James says, "By being religious we establish ourselves in possession of ultimate reality at the only points at which reality is given us to guard. Our responsible concern is with our private destiny, after all" (394–395). The whole point of "The Will to Believe" was to say that that we do not have to settle the question of whether our beliefs correspond to reality, much less whether they put us in possession of ultimate reality, in order to have a right to beliefs that do us good.

The central argument of that earlier essay was that when a live, momentous, and forced option cannot be settled by an appeal to evidence, then we have a right to let our emotions decide. There James is clear that whether to be a supernaturalist—whether to believe that we do *not* live on the surface of a frozen lake, because, *pace* natural science, the best things in the universe will throw the last stone—is exactly this sort of option. But in the "Conclusions" to *Varieties* he seems to be saying that this option can and should be settled by evidence—that the experiences of religious virtuosi provide evidence sufficient to make it only rational for naturalists to give up their naturalism. I doubt that he really wanted to pitch it that strongly, but it is hard to construe the argument of that chapter in any other way.

If we do so construe it, then in "Conclusions" James betrays his own pragmatism. For pragmatists, the question of when evidence can or cannot be used to settle belief is a sociological one: what counts as sufficient evidence is a matter of the consensus of informed inquirers. There is no such consensus in the case of naturalism vs. supernaturalism. James can hardly claim that naturalists like Clifford were unaware of the experiences of the religious virtuosi. So the most James is entitled to conclude from surveying those experiences is that he personally feels reinforced in his attachment to supernaturalism. He is not in a position to say that Clifford has been given reason to think again.

We can, however, avoid construing the "Conclusions" chapter this way by saying that James is arguing not for the existence of God as something outside of the believer, but only for the existence of the believer's subconscious self. So when he says that if we disregard what he calls "over-beliefs," the only "literally and objectively true" belief for which the experiences of the virtuosi give us evidence is that "the conscious person is continuous with a wider self through which saving experiences come" (405), we might (as I suggested earlier) take this in a sense in which that belief would have been perfectly acceptable to a doughty naturalist such as Freud. For Freud's wider self is not a supernatural entity but just the part of the brain that holds the unconscious beliefs and desires that determine the pinch of our individual destinies. This construal is supported by the fact that when James goes on to identify this wider self with "the unseen or mystical world" he explicitly calls this identification his own "over-belief" (405–406). To be consistent with "The Will to Believe," James would have to say that this over-belief is not the sort of thing for which there could be empirical evidence, but that he has a right to it nonetheless.

I conclude that we face the following dilemma in interpreting this chapter: either Freud and James agree on the evidential value of religious experience, or James is betraying his own pragmatism. If we grasp the first horn, then we shall say that all that James can say in reply to Freud's *The Future of an Illusion* is that Freud makes the same mistake as Clifford. He mistakenly infers from the fact that "our ancestors made so many errors of fact and mixed them with their religion" that "we should leave off being religious at all" (394), and therefore fails to recognize our right to whatever religious over-beliefs the pinch of our individual destinies produces. But to grasp this horn is to be left wondering why we need bother with all those virtuosi—whether the twenty Gifford lectures add anything to the twenty pages of "The Will to Believe."

I think the more attractive alternative is to grasp the second horn, and to say that although *Varieties* does indeed betray pragmatism, James was, for better or worse, more than just a pragmatist. I think it was for the worse. This is because I do not—and here I disagree with John McDermott, Hilary Putnam, Bennett Ramsey, David Lamberth, and many other commentators—see anything of value in either *Radical Empiricism* or *A Pluralistic Universe*. I read those books as unpragmatic exercises in Bergsonian metaphysics. The latter enterprise is, in my view, the last feeble gasp of Berkeley's religiously inspired, but utterly wrong-headed, polemic against abstract ideas.[7]

I can, however, happily concede that, unlike those later two books, *The Varieties of Religious Experience* will continue to be read with profit for centuries to come. This is not because it provides good arguments for any particular conclusion, but because it is a portion of the intellectual autobiography of an exceptionally magnanimous man. James's mind was uncommonly capacious, and his charity uncommonly expansive. Reading *Varieties* can help us become more like James, and thus help us become better people.

NOTES

1. Unless otherwise indicated, all parenthetical page references are to William James, *The Varieties of Religious Experience* (Cambridge: Harvard University Press, 1985).

2. John Dewey, *The Later Works, 1925–1953*, 17 vols., ed. Jo Ann Boydston et al. (Carbondale: Southern Illinois University Press, 1981–1990), 9:56.

3. Ibid. 9.

4. Ibid. 10.

5. Ibid. 13.

6. James, confusingly enough, sometimes describes what we call pragmatism as empiricism. Thus at 361 of *Varieties* he describes "the empirical philosophy" as the view that "the true is what works well." At 350, in the course of a brief reprise of "Philosophical Conceptions and Practical Results," he says that "the guiding principle of British philosophy has in fact been that every difference must make a difference."

7. As Peirce's review of Fraser's edition of Berkeley shows, Berkeley's polemic can be read as a sort of proto-pragmatism, as well as an anticipation of the metaphysics of raw feeling. But Peirce had no hostility to abstract ideas, only a wish to give them ontological status through his doctrine of the reality of Thirdness. James may have thought of the pragmatist reduction of such ideas to their effects upon conduct and the Bergsonian repudiation of them in favor of "intuition" as bound up with each other. As I see it, however, that repudiation was a misfortune, for it delayed acceptance of what Bergmann called "the linguistic turn," a turn that Peirce, in his later writings, helped us to take.

6

A Pragmatist's Progress

The Varieties of James's Strategies for Defending Religion

PHILIP KITCHER

I

*F*or all its richness of psychological description, William
James's *Varieties of Religious Experience* can easily engender philosophical disappointment. James's ostensible purpose
is the validation of religious experience, a task that seems to be
announced throughout the earlier lectures, although his treatment of it is partial and qualified with "repeated postpone-
ments."[1] At the beginning of Lectures XVI and XVII, devoted
to mysticism, James tells us that push has come to shove, and
that he intends to convince his reader "of the reality of the
states in question [mystical states], and of the paramount importance of their function."[2] From the very beginning of *Varieties*, individual religious experience has been seen as the heart
of religion, and earlier discussions are regarded as showing that
"personal religious experience has its root and center in mystical states of consciousness."[3] The natural reading of the tanta-
lizingly vague language about the "reality" of mystical states is
to suppose that James now intends to argue that mystical states

are indicators of a reality—"transcendent" reality—that cannot be apprehended in other ways.

That reading is natural because it is so hard to understand what *else* James might have in mind. Suppose, for example, we were to read the claim "Mystical states are real" as asserting only that there is a class of psychological states in which people sometimes find themselves, a class picked out by the expression "mystical states." So inoffensive a thesis hardly seems to need argument, or to merit advertisement as the main tenet of a long book. Moreover, if we take the crucial issue to be that of determining whether or not mystical states can provide the subject with knowledge of transcendent reality—whether or not they are *veridical*— then it's possible to interpret *Varieties* as a "long argument" (in Darwin's famous phrase)[4] for a conclusion in which James was clearly much interested. If the varieties of religious experience can be understood in terms of the genesis of psychological states that occur in their purest forms in the lives of mystics, and if these pure forms can serve as sources of religious knowledge, then it will be possible to defend the thesis that religious people have experiences that yield a core of religious knowledge, even though they may sometimes, perhaps always, surround that core with the mistaken doctrines that differentiate creeds and sects. The natural reading commends itself to us because the only alternative seems trivial and because it gives a structure to the argument of *Varieties* that seems to align itself with James's enduring predilections.

To adopt the natural reading is, however, to set James up for a bad fall. How could one hope to argue that mystical states reliably indicate characteristics of transcendent reality? That cannot be done in the ways in which we validate the capacities of people with unusual powers— those with perfect pitch, with the ability to identify the year and vintage of the wine, with the knack of identifying the day on which some past date fell, and so forth. In cases like these we have independent access to truth values of the claims that the talented subjects deliver, by observing the pitches that are struck on the piano, the label on the bottle, or the relevant part of the calendar. With respect to mystical states, there is no such alternative avenue to the alleged reality that the subjects are detecting, and, indeed, if there were, James's brief for the centrality of mystical experience would collapse. The only hope, then, would seem to lie in the suggestion that the best explanation of the occurrence of the states would take them to be veridical. Unfortunately, James, experienced psychologist that he is, is fully aware of rival possibilities for explaining the presence of mystical states, emphasizing throughout *Varieties* the potential role of unconscious psychodynamic processes ("whole systems of underground life") and directly connecting the experiences of mystics to states induced by alcohol, anesthetics, and intoxicants.[5] So, according to the available evidence, which he dutifully records, mystical states may well be caused by processes that regularly, even invariably, distort our judgments and give rise to illusions and hallucinations. In consequence, he can hardly claim that the veridicality of mystical states is part of the best explanation of their occurrence. If anything, an explanation that assimilates them to delusions looks more promising, although the prudent verdict might well be that there is no basis for resolving the question.

The line of reasoning just rehearsed is so simple and uncomplicated that no philosopher as astute as James could possibly miss it. The natural reading thus attributes to *Varieties* an argumentative structure that can only succeed if a particular project is completed, and then construes James's attempt to complete that project as vitiated by a blatant blunder. My aim in what follows is to develop a different interpretation of the philosophical role of *Varieties*. I'll begin by deepening my critique of the natural reading, first by looking more closely at some of James's apparent validations of religious experience in *Varieties*, and second by exposing the peculiarity of viewing the author of "The Will to Believe" as engaged in the enterprise of identifying sources of religious knowledge.

II

Once he has outlined "the general traits of the mystic range of consciousness," James turns to what the natural reading identifies as the critical question.

> My next task is to inquire whether we can invoke it [mystical experience] as authoritative. Does it furnish any *warrant for the truth* of the twice-bornness and supernaturality and pantheism which it favors?[6]

He immediately presents his answer, in three-part form:

1. Mystical states, when well developed, usually are, and have the right to be, absolutely authoritative over the individuals to whom they come.

2. No authority emanates from them which should make it a duty for those who stand outside of them to accept their revelations uncritically.

3. They break down the authority of the nonmystical or rationalistic consciousness, based upon the understanding and the senses alone. They show it to be only one kind of consciousness. They open out the possibility of other orders of truth, in which, so far as anything in us vitally responds to them, we may freely continue to have faith.[7]

These answers make it appear as though James is in a complete muddle.

Consider (1), ignoring the vague hedge about "well-developed" states. Part of it consists of an unobjectionable psychological generalization: people who have had what they characterize as mystical experiences will typically conceive those experiences to be indicators of transcendent reality. The epistemological sting comes with James's claim that they have the right to do so. How do they come to have this right? On the face of it, they can identify themselves as having undergone psychological processes that induce states of belief, and can recognize that there is no independent standard for judging the frequency with which processes of these types generate true beliefs. It would therefore seem reasonable for them to wonder if the voices they hear or the visions they see are different from the hallucinations of the drug taker or the delusions of the mentally ill.

One way to develop this line of criticism is to inquire how James can simultaneously advance his three theses. Suppose one could garner evidence for claiming that mystical states were veridical. Then, of course, there'd be no difficulty in understanding how the subjects of such states have the right to take them to be authoritative, but, by the same token, others, less fortunate in their more limited experiences, ought to defer to those with broader capacities, in the same way that the color-blind subordinate their judgments about the colors of traffic lights. If there's evidence for the veridical character of mystical states, then James can maintain (1) but not (2). On the other hand, if our epistemic situation is one in which there is a genuine doubt about the veridicality of mystical states,[8] it would seem that the clear-headed mystic, aware of this situation, ought to suspend judgment about what the states disclose, however forceful and vivid those states may seem. That would allow for the assertion of (2) and (3)—for there is, of course, the *possibility* of "other orders of truth" (or better: other sources of knowledge)—but it would be at odds with (1). James seems to be impaled on the horns of a dilemma, with no way to make his three answers consistent.

The best response to this dilemma would be to take advantage of the difference between the notion of *right* that figures in (1) and that of *duty*, which we find in (2). Suppose James were to insist that background knowledge of the ways in which belief formation can go awry is not pertinent, proposing instead that what matters is the actual reliability of the processes that the mystics undergo. Their having the right to believe the things they do would now turn on whether the processes that induce their special beliefs actually generate true beliefs with high frequency. On this line of interpretation, outsiders can have the right to believe the mystical conclusions, for they can acquire the habit of tracking the mystics' utterances and acquiescing in them, and, if they do so, they will form beliefs by means of reliable processes, thus satisfying the standard for having the right to believe. Hence a construal that allows rights to believe to come relatively easily, so as to make (1) true, also gives outsiders a *right* to accept the mystics' revelations, but it will not impose a *duty* unless subjects are required to undergo any reliable belief-forming processes that are available to them. At this point, however, James can reasonably suggest that duties only arise when the reliability of the belief-forming processes can be identified, and that, in cases where the evidence is insufficient for us to gauge the frequency with which a particular process generates true beliefs, we have no obligation to undergo that process and acquire the beliefs that it generates. This method of evading the dilemma plainly recapitulates important themes of "The Will to Believe," for, in both instances, the strategy is to claim permissibility even though there is no obligation to direct one's doxastic life in a particular direction.

There is, however, an obvious difficulty. Even if James can escape the charge of inconsistency, all that has been shown is that, on the interpretation of rights and duties proposed, it is *possible* that all three of James's theses are true. Whether that possibility is actualized turns on the reliability of mystical experience—and we might note that, if the question is resolved in favor of (1), then not only is (3) unnecessarily weak but the resolution would provide just that identification of the reliability of a type of process that would bridge the gap between rights and duties. So, if James could provide convincing grounds for (1), he'd show that mystical experiences are reliable guides to transcendent reality, thereby giving the outsider grounds for deferring to the mystics—effectively showing that outsiders should view mystics as analogous to those with absolute pitch—and he'd thus undercut (2). Hence James faces what looks like a pragmatic paradox: he is committed to asserting something of the form "*p* but I have no good grounds for asserting *p*."

James's efforts at defending (1) are as unconvincing as they are brief. He presents his case in two sentences.

> Our own more "rational" beliefs are based on evidence exactly similar in nature to that which mystics quote for theirs. Our senses, namely, have assured us of certain states of fact; but mystical experiences are as direct perceptions of fact for those who have them as any sensations were for us.[9]

The obvious response to this passage is to accuse James of begging crucial questions in his claims about the similarity of mystical experience and ordinary perception. He writes as if skepticism about mystical experience would commit us to skepticism about ordinary perceptual experience. Whether or not one can find an adequate answer to Cartesian concerns about all our experience, there are everyday practices of validating knowledge claims, practices we use to explore the conditions under which various forms of perceptual experience are reliable. Through these practices we validate some kinds of perceptual processes, show that others are unreliable, and obtain only inconclusive results with respect to the rest. Thus we differentiate the experiences of alert, sober observers who look at stationary objects in good light from those of people stupefied by drink who are trying to track fast-moving things in the twilight; and, at various stages in the history of inquiry, we wonder if various extensions of our senses, paradigmatically scientific instruments, can be trusted to generate correct conclusions. Perhaps in the future we might be able to arrive at a more determinate judgment about mystical experiences—positively if the mystic were to deliver verifiably correct answers to hard factual questions, negatively if neuropsychological inquiries revealed fine-grained similarities between mystical states and drug-induced conditions—but, for the present, we have to regard the mystics' claims as simply uncheckable. In the spirit of James's (3), we might allow the possibility that they provide avenues to aspects of reality we cannot ordinarily apprehend, but we can't give them the same endorsement we assign to ordinary perceptual experience.

So far, I've been treating *Varieties* as if its epistemological project were couched in the terms of contemporary analytic epistemology, and, so regarded, it appears to fail dismally.[10] Yet my casual references to truth, left unexplained in previous discussions, should have sounded an alarm. James is well known for having urged an approach to truth that is a rival to—or, perhaps, a deeper explication of—the conception of truth as correspondence to reality.[11] According to the famous slogan in which he encapsulated his position,

> "The true," to put it very briefly, is only the expedient in the way of our thinking, just as "the right" is only the expedient in our way of behaving. Expedient in almost any fashion; and expedient in the long run and on the whole of course; for what meets expediently all the experience in sight won't necessarily meet all farther experiences equally satisfactorily.[12]

It would be unwise to assume that James in 1902 already had clearly in mind the views about truth that he would articulate in 1907, but there are obvious respects in which the emphasis on expedience makes sense of discussions of religious experience in *Varieties*.

We can start from the conclusions on which I have been focusing and on aspects of James's formulation that I have left out of the picture. Note first that thesis (3) juxtaposes the idea of "orders of truth" with a reference to the subject's reaction; James adds the clause "so far as anything in us vitally responds to them." Perhaps we could explain this away by supposing that he is separating the properly epistemological issue ("Do mystical experiences reliably induce beliefs that correspond to some transcendent reality?") from the pragmatic issue as to whether these are aspects of reality in which human beings are interested. The slogan about truth suggests an alternative reading, to wit, that the criterion by which mystical experiences are to be judged has nothing to do with correspondence to reality, but is rather a matter of the expedience of the beliefs induced for the subject who acquires them. In the same way, as we read on and encounter James's defense of (1), the two-sentence epistemological argument I have criticized is preceded by what appears to be a psychological account of the difficulty of convincing mystics—including the rhetorical question, "If the mystical truth that comes to a man proves to be a force that he can live by, what mandate have we of the majority to order him to live in another way?"[13] Again, one can try to separate epistemological from pragmatic questions, reading James as asking why we should give priority to truth over other values (where truth is understood in a correspondence sense), or we can take the connection between "mystical truth" and "a force one can live by" to be tighter. Read in the light of the slogan James would offer five years later, both passages suggest the possibility that the authority of mystical experiences is to be assessed, not by canvassing the frequency with which they generate beliefs that correspond to (transcendent) reality, but by appraising their tendency to induce attitudes that are expedient for those who undergo the experiences.

One of the most obvious recurrent features of *Varieties* is its exploration of the ways in which religious experiences play a positive role in people's lives. Numerous discussions of the experiences of individual subjects consider the possibilities of psychological explanations in terms of natural mechanisms, some of them unconscious, juxtaposing these scientific approaches to the phenomena with an inquiry into the "fruits for life." I shall focus on two representative examples.

In his exploration of cases of religious conversion, James poses for himself the same kind of critical question we have encountered in the discussion of mysticism: "May the whole phenomenon of regeneration, even in these startling instantaneous examples, possibly be a strictly natural process, divine in its fruits, of course, but in one case more and in another less so, and neither more nor less divine in its mere causation and mechanism than any other process, high or low, of man's interior life?"[14] His immediate response is to outline for his readers the possibilities of unconscious causes of psychological phenomena (and here James is obviously impressed with late nineteenth-century work in psychology),[15] thus underscoring the possibility that experiences that are hard to explain involve "incursions" from the unconscious, and may be akin to "obsessive ideas, or even hallucinations of sight or hearing."[16] But then he appears to switch the standard for evaluating the cases of conversion he has described, and to introduce considerations that foreshadow the idea that the mark of truth is expedience.

> Our spiritual judgment, I said, our opinion of the significance and value of a human event or condition, must be decided on empirical grounds exclusively. If the *fruits for life* of the state of conversion are good, we ought to idealize and venerate it, even though it be a piece of natural psychology; if not, we ought to make short work with it, no matter what supernatural being may have infused it.[17]

It's obviously tempting to suppose that James evades the difficulties that seem to arise for the validation of religious experience by rejecting the standard terms of epistemological debate—effectively insisting that the reliability of religious experience, measured by the frequency with which such experience generates beliefs true in some correspondence sense, is not the crucial issue—proposing instead that the appropriate criterion concerns the ways in which the beliefs induced by the experiences are expedient for those who acquire them. This reading, the *simple pragmatist* reading, will give point to James's many poignant descriptions of examples in which the wreckage of an individual life is salvaged and refashioned through religious conversion.[18]

Simple pragmatism also appears to make sense of James's discussion of saintliness and its value. He begins the three lectures on saintliness by formulating his goal as attaining "a spiritual judgment as to the total value and positive meaning of all the religious trouble and happiness which we have seen."[19] The enterprise receives a more extensive and precise characterization in the following lectures on the value of saintliness.

> What I then propose to do is, briefly stated, to test saintliness by common sense, to use human standards to help us decide how far the religious life commends itself as an ideal kind of human activity. If it commends itself, then any theological beliefs that may inspire it, in so far forth will stand accredited. If not, then they will be discredited, and all without reference to anything but human working principles. It is but the elimination of the humanly unfit, and the survival of the humanly fittest, applied to religious beliefs; and if we look at history candidly and without prejudice, we have to admit that no religion has ever in the long run established or proved itself in any other way.[20]

Having set the stage for his quasi-Darwinian investigation, James brings before his reader a cast of saints or "spiritual heroes," appraising their successes not in biological terms but by considering the "larger environment of history," and he concludes that "the saintly group of qualities is indispensable to the world's welfare."[21] This conclusion is qualified by vocabulary similar to that which he employs in stating the pragmatist view of truth, reinforcing the thought that we have been offered a validation of religious experience through the demonstration of its expedience in the way of belief.[22]

Yet there are plenty of indications that simple pragmatism cannot be James's whole story. He is plainly aware of the obvious objection that, while a comforting illusion might make a subject feel happier or convert a drunkard into a model citizen, thus being in a certain sense "expedient in the way of belief," it would be an abuse of language to assess the consoling or inspirational belief as true. Indeed, he presents the objection himself, both at the beginning of his investigation and at the stage when he has announced his apparently triumphant conclusion. Here is the first formulation.

> Abstractly, it would seem illogical to try to measure the worth of a religion's fruits in merely human terms of value. How *can* you measure their worth without considering whether the God really exists who is supposed to inspire them?[23]

The most challenging version of the objection, not precisely formulated by James in the discussion that immediately follows, would present an intuitive view about human well-being. Imagine a person who believes a consoling falsehood, supposing that plans and projects dear to her are successful, whereas, in reality, they go badly awry and the dreary truth is kept from her only through an elaborate deception. It would be shallow to suppose that this person's belief was expedient or that its fruits for her life were good. Even though the alternative course of her life might be less happy, there is a natural impulse to feel that her well-being might be enhanced were she to face the actual situation and do what she can to improve it.[24] By the same token, a devout Christian whose gloomy fears are dissipated with the thought of personal salvation has only adopted the genuinely "expedient in the way of belief" if both the deity and the promise of redemption are real. Even James's reformed drunks whose lives are full of good works among the poor do not show that specifically *religious* beliefs are expedient, unless their transformation could not have been achieved through the adoption of beliefs lacking the erroneous theological components, beliefs about the damaging effects of strong liquors and the rightness of aiding those in need.

Although James follows the passage just cited by taking up a less forceful objection (essentially one concerned with the credentials of religions that are now regarded as demanding cruel and unnecessary practices), he clearly does not think he has settled all doubts about his strategy of appraising religious experiences by considering their "fruits for life." After announcing his conclusion about the "successes" of saintly lives, he offers a discussion that appears to distinguish sharply between truth and expedience.

> How, you say, can religion, which believes in two worlds and an invisible order, be estimated by the adaptation of its fruits to this order alone? It is its *truth*, not its utility, you insist, upon which our verdict ought to depend. If religion is true, its fruits are good fruits, even though in this world, they should prove uniformly ill adapted and full of naught but pathos. It goes back, then, after all, to the question of the truth of theology.[25]

Moreover, it is exactly at this point in the text that James announces his readiness to address the crucial issue and to take up the veridicality of mystical states. Simple pragmatism cannot, therefore, be the correct reading of *Varieties*, for if it were simply a matter of judging the expedience of religious belief and measuring expedience by the kinds of psychological effects that James has taken such pains to describe, his task would now be done. Instead, he launches into the confusing (and apparently confused) arguments I reviewed at the beginning of this section.

To make further progress, we can find clues at the very end of the lectures on mysticism, where James is offering his comments on part (3) of his tripartite answer. There he tells us that mystical states do not "deny anything on which our senses have seized."[26] Explicitly judging that there is no evidential basis for accepting or rejecting the reliability of mystical states ("It must always remain an open question whether mystical states may not possibly be such superior points of view, windows through which the mind looks out on a more extensive and inclusive world"), he suggests that we transcend the attempt to classify them as cases of knowledge or as delusions: "They offer us *hypotheses*, hypotheses which we may voluntarily ignore, but which as thinkers we cannot possibly upset."[27] These passages resonate with other, very familiar, parts of James's philosophical corpus. They point us back to "The Will to Believe."[28]

III

Written as a response to W. K. Clifford's essay "The Ethics of Belief," James's famous address takes for granted that he and his opponent share a commonplace of post-Darwinian, eminent Victorian intellectuals: there is no such thing as religious *knowledge.* James and Clifford are thoroughly aware that the going picture of the natural world is hardly sympathetic to the thesis of a providential deity. They recognize that a century's worth of "higher criticism" has identified the seams in the major religious texts of the western world. Nascent anthropological investigations have disclosed the extraordinary diversity of religious belief—to the extent that James's "Circumscription of the Topic" will only find at the core of religion a gesture toward the "transcendent."[29] Having read his Hegel, James is fully aware of the philosophical problems of identifying a "given" in any kind of experience.[30] Hence the issue he debates with Clifford concerns the permissibility of believing where one does not know, where the evidence is (and must remain) insufficient for knowledge. Grown-up late Victorians realize that religion must discard any pretensions to knowledge; their question concerns the legitimacy of faith.

Surely, then, the natural reading of *Varieties* must be wrong. Only if he were the Don Quixote of philosophy would James desert the more sophisticated perspective of his younger self and attempt to show that, after all, there is a way of defending the reliability of religious experiences and so identifying genuine religious *knowledge.* We have seen that when the pertinent passages in *Varieties* are construed as essaying that style of defense they involve blatant errors. The natural reading compels us to write off *Varieties* (insofar as we treat it as a philosophical work) as the overreaching of a very confused thinker, who abandons his earlier insight (no religious knowledge; religion is to be validated by showing the permissibility of belief in the absence of evidence) in the hope of achieving a more ambitious thesis. But James was not so befuddled. As the concluding section of the lectures on mysticism, advertised as the crux of the book, makes clear with its talk of "open questions," "hypotheses," and "voluntary" assent, the perspective of "The Will to Believe" is implicit in the later work.[31]

If, as I propose, we read *Varieties* through the lens of the earlier address, then we shall need an overview of its central claims (consideration of the main arguments will come later), together with some appreciation of the respects in which James's earlier treatment of the permissibility of religious faith might need to be supplemented. I begin with an obvious, but important, point: despite the fact that both Clifford and James are principally interested in the legitimacy of *religious* belief that outruns the evidence, their discussions are formulated in general terms. Clifford attempts to argue that "it is wrong always, everywhere, and for anyone, to believe anything upon insufficient evidence";[32] James counters by arguing that our "passional nature" not only does, but in some cases *may* and even *must* play a role in the formation of our beliefs.[33] His discussion raises many interesting epistemological points, some of which we shall consider in later sections. For the moment, however, I want to show how the challenge to Clifford's Principle only outlines a case for the permissibility of religious faith.

James is very clear that he must overcome resistance to the idea of willing oneself to believe: "Does it not seem preposterous on the very face of it to talk of our opinions being modifiable at will?"[34] He tries to defuse the sense of strangeness by offering an interpretation of Pascal's Wager; Pascal did not offer the crass suggestion that consideration of the utilities of belief and denial would induce faith, but rather that obtaining a clear view of the gamble would prompt a rational subject to undertake those devotional practices, spiritual exercises, out of which faith would eventually come. In the light of *Varieties*, the argument can be elaborated further, for James's cast of characters, his mystics, converted and reformed sinners, and his sick souls, all have an inclination, in many cases an overpowering one, to form beliefs with religious content. If, in line with the discussion of the last section, we concede that to acquire the beliefs would be to outrun the evidence, indeed to outrun any potential evidence, then it is clear that the question isn't one of working to engender a new belief but rather that of allowing the operation of tendencies the subjects already have.

Clifford advances his principle to recommend the inhibition of the natural inclinations of the kinds of subjects who populate *Varieties*. If the principle is correct, then these people are guilty of moral errors. James replies that the grounds for the principle are one-sided, focusing on one type of mistake and omitting from consideration an equally important possibility of going astray, for Clifford has failed to see that acquiring true belief is an important desideratum for us and we are not solely concerned to avoid error. Obsessed with the badness of coming to believe something that is false, he does not recognize that it is also bad not to come to believe what is true. This general point is supplemented with a description of instances in which the inhibition of belief in accordance with Clifford's Principle would deprive the subject of a genuine good. Here James offers the examples of moral commitments and the beliefs about other people that facilitate personal relations, both intimate and broadly social: a lover's passionate conviction, beyond the evidence, may win the beloved, and our everyday trust in the cooperation of others may promote the smooth operation of our polity. I shall return to the merits of these arguments in the next section. For the moment, let us assume that they suffice to undermine Clifford's Principle, and inquire after the consequences for the religious case.

James takes up the permissibility of religious faith in the final section of "The Will to Believe," and it has to be conceded that this is the weakest part of his essay. Trouble begins with his sensitivity to religious diversity.[35] In a brief prefiguring of Lecture II of *Varieties* ("Circumscription of the Topic"), he tells us that the "religious hypothesis" consists of two parts, the first declaring that "the best things are the eternal things" and the second maintaining that we are better off if we believe the first part. Given this way of characterizing religion, James has an easy time contending that, if the hypothesis turns out to be true, we are going to lose something good by failing to believe it—for that is written into the second part. Hence he can assimilate the case of religion to the arguments he has previously launched against Clifford's Principle, insisting on the losses that come from failing to believe what is true and from worrying compulsively about avoiding error.

There are, however, three related objections to this facile argument. The first is that it's not at all obvious that James's religious hypothesis has any content: does he mean that the best things are simply the eternal things? And what exactly are those? Presumably James would not want to count some empty region of Newtonian space as one of the "best things," even supposing that that region were to last forever. Nor do his glosses help to explain what he has in mind, for he speaks of the "more eternal" things as "the overlapping things, the things in the universe that throw the last stone, so to speak, and say the final word."[36] It's hard to think of the constituent phrases as possessing anything like their customary meaning, and, in consequence, reasonable to doubt that anything determinate has been said. Second, even if one concedes that James's "religious hypothesis" has a sense, it seems highly unlikely that it captures what the religious believer wants to endorse. Superficially, at least, opponents of the most prominent religions could sign on to James's hypothesis by offering their own, deviant construals of "the more eternal things"—humanists, for example, might take these to be the individual and collective achievements of our species. The devout are likely to be disappointed if all they are to receive is license to embrace so thin a doctrine, for their interest will probably lie in the permissibility of believing in a providential deity or in a possible progression of the soul through a sequence of lives toward some privileged final state. Indeed, James himself doesn't rest content with the official formulation of the "religious hypothesis," and it's not long before he offers a more ambitious gloss:

> This feeling, forced on us we know not whence, that by obstinately believing that there are gods (although not to do so would be easy for our logic and our life) we are doing the universe the deepest service we can, seems part of the living essence of the religious hypothesis.[37]

Surely not as James has defined that hypothesis, but, though the plural reference may jar the sensibilities of orthodox monotheists, he is plainly elaborating his original spare formulation in ways that religious people are likely to find congenial, even though they may wonder what doing any kind of service to the universe would amount to (and despite the fact that readers of *Varieties* may question the view that a godless life is "easy").

The third obvious difficulty with James's defense of the permissibility of religious belief stems from the parallel between his argument and Pascal's Wager. A standard objection to the wager is that there are alternative gambles that promise infinite rewards only to those who believe in different deities or who deliberately refrain from believing in certain deities (perhaps even in all). Consider various hypotheses that are similar to James's official "religious hypothesis": (A) "The Christian God exists and is the most perfect being, and we are better off if we believe this"; (B) "The idea of the Christian God is anathema to the most perfect beings that exist, and we are better off if we believe this (and consequently reject the Christian God)"; (C) "Among the most perfect things are those people who never believe any religious doctrine on insufficient evidence, and we are better off for believing this." With respect to all three "religious hypotheses," we could mimic James's argument for his own, for the formulations assure us that if (A), say, is true, then we are better off believing it, and similarly in the other cases. Since (A) and (B) are incompatible, we are unable to believe both, so we cannot regard belief in either as a "free move" that brings us a possible gain and no possible loss. Perhaps, in the spirit of the passage from Fitz James Stephen that James quotes at the very end of his essay, we should see ourselves as committed to a blind choice between (A) and (B), one that we must make and hope for the best, like the travelers on the mountain pass "in the midst of blinding snow and whirling mist."[38] That, however, would be to ignore the possibility that (C) is true, and that the most humanly profitable strategy is to abstain from judgment. At this point, it is evident that James's attempt to provide us with a religious hypothesis vindicated by his critique of Clifford, that is, a hypothesis we may permissibly believe on insufficient evidence because there are good grounds for thinking that failure to believe it will involve us in a loss, has failed to advance his cause a single step. Assuming his diagnosis of the problems with Clifford's Principle is right, he needs to argue that religious belief is one of the examples that fit the exceptions he has specified, and his attempt to provide that argument collapses.

I suspect James knew that his official argument was scholastic legerdemain, for in his penultimate paragraph, before the closing trope from Stephen, he presents the issue as it surely moved him.

> When I look at the religious question as it really puts itself to concrete men, and when I think of all the possibilities which both practically and theoretically it involves, then this command that we shall put a stopper on our heart, instincts, and courage, and *wait*—acting

of course meanwhile more or less as if religion were *not* true—till
doomsday, or till such time as our intellect and senses working together may have raked in evidence enough—this command, I say,
seems to me the queerest idol ever manufactured in the philosoph-
ic cave.[39]

It would be absurd to think that James's "concrete men" want permission
to believe his official religious hypothesis, or that belief in that hypothesis might make some serious difference to their action—how would they
redirect their lives in accordance with the idea that "the more eternal
things are perfect" or with the injunction to "serve the universe"? What
these people want, what James himself wants, is the permissibility of
those religious beliefs to which our heart, instincts, and courage incline
us, and this is not what the (flawed) argument he has just rehearsed could
hope to deliver. As a defense of religion, then, "The Will to Believe" is
radically incomplete.

Nonetheless, the essay does open up the *possibility* of a defense. Clifford has been deprived of his principle, the cudgel with which he hoped
to belabor the faithful, and James has tried to argue that there are situations in which believing something on insufficient evidence has good
consequences. The closing section of "The Will to Believe" goes astray
because it attempts to short-circuit the hard work of demonstrating that
belief in religious doctrines can have the same kind of good consequences—in effect, James tries to gerrymander the religious doctrine so
that the point about good consequences will come for free—but the
issue ultimately requires a vast amount of empirical detail. The sentence
just quoted, about the problem as it presents itself to "concrete men,"
hints at the sort of empirical case James envisages as possible: to with-
hold belief is, he intimates, to do a kind of violence to ourselves, to dam
up our natural tendencies and inclinations. Perhaps, then, we need a
fuller study of religious belief, one that would show how religion responds to important aspects of the human predicament, how coming to
believe can satisfy yearnings that would otherwise lead people to despair, how belief can turn their lives in profitable directions, sometimes
making of those lives, for all their hardship and physical pain, remarkable successes when judged from the broader perspective of history.
Maybe we ought to develop an analysis of the human temperament (or

temperaments) that will reveal the sickness felt by some souls, the fruits of conversion, of saintliness, and of mystical states. Perhaps we need *Varieties*.

<h2 style="text-align:center">IV</h2>

I have only *sketched* my main interpretative claim, to wit, that *Varieties* is set within the epistemological framework of "The Will to Believe" and that it tries to discharge the function of the quick-and-dirty closing section of the earlier essay. To make this claim more precise, and, eventually, to assess James's efforts at defending religious belief, I shall need a much more careful analysis of the issues that arise in his debate with Clifford. For I have simply *assumed* that James correctly diagnoses flaws in Clifford's Principle and that the upshot of his diagnosis requires us to evaluate the consequences of religious belief. Let us proceed more slowly.

Clifford introduces his principle by describing two cases, the more famous of which concerns a ship owner who believes, on insufficient evidence, that one of his vessels is seaworthy. The holding of such a belief, Clifford suggests, is a moral mistake, even if the owner should be lucky and the voyage prove uneventful. Generalizing from examples like these, Clifford arrives at the principle, and an uncharitable reaction to his inference would charge it with just that tolerance of insufficient evidence that the principle castigates. The response is uncharitable because it overlooks Clifford's efforts—admittedly brief—to offer general reasons in support of his principle. Those reasons take the form of insisting that a person's beliefs do not simply affect the actions the person performs but also modify the attitudes of others, so that Clifford views adopting beliefs on insufficient evidence as a kind of infection that may ultimately blight the health of the human community.[40]

Philosophers have been sharply divided about Clifford's Principle: Peter van Inwagen contends that it is straightforwardly false, while Allen Wood mounts a vigorous defense of it.[41] Because that defense brings out the most important features of Clifford's position, it's useful to begin with Wood's reconstruction.

According to Wood, Clifford is concerned with the actions subjects take in forming and regulating their beliefs, and he is interested in whether we should acquiesce in or resist those inclinations that James would take to be natural to us. As Wood sees very clearly, the idea of a moral critique of someone's behavior in this area of her life plainly makes sense, so that one cannot simply dismiss Clifford's Principle by denying that belief formation and belief maintenance are subject to moral appraisal. But it is worth asking after the sources of any moral principle that could apply here, and it appears that there are two possibilities: to suppose that there is an absolute duty to accommodate one's beliefs to the evidence or to suppose that the principle is grounded in the promotion of good consequences. Recognizing that James's principal attacks on Clifford advert to the advantages of sometimes going beyond the evidence, Wood opts for the view that we have a duty to conform to the principle, a duty that derives from broader duties to humanity ("as a community of inquiry") and to ourselves (in terms of fostering our own autonomy).[42] Here I think he goes astray.

Clifford belonged to a group of high-minded Victorians (including T. H. Huxley and John Tyndall) who frequently wrote and talked as if scientific inquiry had rightly inherited the mantle of orthodox religion— and, indeed, it is hardly surprising that their contemporary Francis Galton, Charles Darwin's cousin, seriously characterized scientists as a secular priesthood. If one reads Clifford against the background of the science boosterism common among this group, it is easy to conceive of him as claiming a human duty to the truth so strong that the search for truth can never be subordinated to other considerations. Yet the resultant position is surely monstrous, for it ignores the fact that we have further duties, specifically to advance the welfare of other human beings. If it is possible for those duties to conflict, for there to be situations in which honoring the duty to truth would require actions incompatible with honoring the duty to human welfare, it would appear that the conflict would have to be resolved by appealing to the expected consequences. The alternative supposes that there is some higher-order principle that explains when the duty to truth is to be abrogated under conditions of conflict. If there are *no* such conditions, then we do have the monstrous scientism to which Clifford and his friends sometimes seem to be attracted, which refuses ever to override the duty to truth even in the interests of humanity. If there are such conditions, then, strictly speaking, Clifford's Principle is at best an approximation, something that should bind us when our other duties do not interfere. Finally, if the conflict is to be resolved on consequentialist grounds, then *contra* Wood, James's strategy of attacking Clifford's Principle is fundamentally right.

But there is something more deeply wrong with the idea that Clifford's Principle articulates a duty that descends from the overriding importance of our collective pursuit of truth. It is not simply that we have other values besides truth, but, as James saw, that value judgments are themselves integral to our practice of inquiry. The point can best be made by imagining a philosopher Clifford* who really is prepared to insist on the primacy of our duty to the truth. When James confronts him with hypothetical examples in which human well-being is sacrificed on a broad scale so that the project of human inquiry can be advanced, Clifford* does not flinch, but replies that the sufferings are an unfortunate price that must be paid for pursuing the goal that most fully expresses our human nature.[43] We now ask for a fuller specification of this end, so that we may appreciate its enormous importance—what exactly is it that this project of inquiry can be expected to deliver? Truths, of course—but we know in advance that it cannot provide *all* of them, and we are curious to know the character of those that will be forthcoming. Clifford* will tell us that inquiry aims at disclosing the "fundamental" truths, the "significant" ones, but the simple flashing of these labels should not close the conversation. What makes some truths "fundamental" or "significant"—in ways that make the discovery of them more important than other human endeavors? Value judgments lie behind Clifford*'s response, and, James will argue, when those value judgments are made explicit, we shall see that not all the values involved are epistemic.[44]

So far, I have presented the considerations against Clifford's Principle in a very general way, but it's possible to develop further the kinds of examples that James uses in "The Will to Believe." Imagine a person who is diagnosed as having a rare form of cancer; the available statistics present an extremely discouraging picture, in that all known patients have died within two years of diagnosis. Despite his firm grasp of statistics, the patient acquires the strong conviction that he will be different, and this positive attitude actually contributes to a recovery and a life of two more decades.[45] We can even extend the example: the person is a uniquely talented contributor to the projects Clifford holds most dear, the advancement of inquiry and the maintenance of a society marked by the free flow of information and open, critical discussion. Finally, to guard against any concern that the patient's attitudes will serve as some source of intellectual rot, we'll assume that nobody else ever knows that he has come to believe, in the absence of sufficient evidence, that he will recover.

If it is wrong always and everywhere for anyone to believe anything on the basis of insufficient evidence, then the patient has made a moral error. If Clifford's Principle is true, then, despite all the good consequences, from the twenty years' survival to the accomplishments that revolutionize inquiry and spread broadly the goods of knowledge and vigorous debate, we have to condemn the wishful thinking that generated the goods. The imagined duty to truth must be so strong that it overrides any pleading about good effects, even though the effects centrally involve the very good, truth, that figures in the duty. I suggested earlier that a rigid insistence on duty could easily appear monstrous, and the present example brings out the features that make most people find such rigid insistence unattractive.[46] Moreover, I doubt that Clifford himself is committed to a policy of duty *über alles* and damn the consequences, for, although his other writings sometimes flirt with a naturalistic (Darwinian) approach to ethics, "The Ethics of Belief" seems to presuppose a form of consequentialism. As I noted earlier, Clifford doesn't simply leap to a very strong generalization from a pair of persuasive examples, but offers general reasons for his principle, and those reasons are straightforwardly consequentialist in character. If we relax the principle, he tells us, we will do a "great wrong to Man" and introduce a "danger to society," where the great wrong is understood in terms of the bad ends of believing what is false and becoming credulous, and the danger is glossed in terms of a society in which interpersonal exchanges are careless about matters of truth. Thus Clifford's consequentialism naturally invites the responses that James gives and that I have extended, responses that introduce other valuable ends and that describe situations in which Clifford's own valued ends can be promoted (without danger) by abrogating the principle.

There is another type of consequentialist example that cuts more deeply at Clifford's Principle. It would be natural, and probably correct, to attribute to Clifford the belief that members of the scientific community are far more likely to live up to his principle than are other members of their societies. Clifford's discussion, however, is pervaded by his insight that inquiry is a community project, that the great end is a community of people among whom knowledge is broadly distributed. Now it is worth asking if the principle is really in accordance with this collective end: specifically, would it be better from the perspective of promoting the kind of society in which Clifford is ultimately interested (marked by broadly distributed knowledge and critical discussion) if the members of that society sometimes violated the principle? I think that the answer is affirmative, partly on grounds articulated by John Stuart Mill,[47] partly because of the contribution that the development of doxastic diversity plays in the advancement of community knowledge. It is very clear from the history of the sciences that great transformations in communitywide knowledge sometimes depend on the laborious efforts of individuals who are prepared to articulate a point of view that appears, for a long time, quite implausible or at best unsupported, in light of the available evidence: Copernicus spent thirty-six years working out the system he eventually published in *De Revolutionibus*, Lavoisier took over a decade before he had convincing evidence to favor the view to which he had been committed, and Darwin's building of the case for evolution under natural selection occupied somewhere between twenty and thirty years. Doctrinaire Cliffordians may insist that it is good if people *pursue* large unsupported ideas, so long as they don't make the moral mistake of actually *believing* them until the sufficient evidence has come in, and they may stick to their guns despite the obvious psychological point that the development of a radically new perspective is more likely if the developer is fully committed to it. The important point, however, is that sermons in favor of detached pursuit are simply silly, given Clifford's actual ends. So long as the scientific community has mechanisms that demand the presentation of sufficient evidence before a novel idea is inscribed "on the books," the individual commitments are harmless. A healthy community will contain not only cautious Cliffordians but also a number of enthusiastic mavericks, ready to endorse new hypotheses that challenge established doctrines and to articulate these hypotheses and the evidence for them. Most of them fail, because they do not present sufficient evidence in the court of scientific opinion, but a tiny minority, who have begun by defying Clifford's Principle and ended by conforming to it, succeed in making some of the largest and most important changes to the collective project of inquiry.[48]

At this point, it is useful to look briefly at van Inwagen's critique of Clifford's Principle. Van Inwagen sees that in many areas of inquiry, specifically in science and in philosophy, people do make up their minds in advance of the evidence, and he appeals to the generality of the phenomenon to urge that it is benign and that Clifford's Principle ought to be rejected.[49] But a critique of Clifford ought not to ignore the consequences the principle is designed to avoid. With respect to van Inwagen's central example, that of the commitments of different philosophers to different metaphysical beliefs, it's easy to explain the liberty of academics to commit themselves passionately, given the presence of safeguards that protect the intellectual polity (and the society) from the creeping rot that Clifford fears. The proliferation of philosophical ideas is valuable because those ideas can open up new ways of thinking, inside and outside the academy, but it would be extraordinary hubris on the part of any partisan of the doctrines van Inwagen considers to think that his opinions were likely to become part of the shared wisdom of society. The moral we ought to draw from van Inwagen's discussion is precisely the one I have suggested in the case of scientific inquiry: Clifford's Principle is directed toward achieving particular goals, chiefly the advancement of knowledge and the fostering of societies in which knowledge is broadly disseminated and in which there is a practice of critical discussion, and the principle ought to be rejected when individual lapses from it would promote those goals (or, perhaps, would not interfere with those goals).

Van Inwagen's treatment is far too cavalier about the larger concerns that move Clifford (in that van Inwagen fails to recognize that the principle is not needed where there are social mechanisms for avoiding the perils Clifford fears). Wood appreciates the force of Clifford's concerns, but he preserves the principle from threatening counterexamples by developing a deontology that makes the principle look monstrous and inhumane. James, I believe, was more nearly correct, seeing that its merits must be assessed on consequentialist grounds and identifying some of the situations in which the consequences tell against it. I now want to develop James's position in a bit more detail so that we can return to the role that *Varieties* plays in the defense of religion.

V

James denies that believing on insufficient evidence invariably promotes a lax attitude toward truth, and at the heart of his response to Clifford is the idea that respect for truth can be expressed in a number of distinct ways. His point can be dramatized by considering two rival societies. The Impulsive have developed an educational policy that instills in their children belief-forming propensities of a more liberal kind than those in force among the Prudent. Thus Jim, a well brought-up Impulsive, has formed in the course of his young life a total of 1,100 distinct beliefs, 100 of which are true and the remaining 1,000 false. His counterpart Cliff, born among the Prudent on exactly the same day as Jim, has received a thoroughly Prudent education that has left him with a much more limited stock of beliefs—just 11, in fact, of which 10 are true and only one false. Cliff looks at Jim with disdain, appalled at the ways in which he believes so much on insufficient evidence. Cliff is visited by an angel, who explains to him the distribution of truth values for both sets of beliefs. Cliff is quietly gratified that Jim's Impulsive ways have led him to so bad a condition, and he judges his own situation to be much preferable. When the angel visits Jim, however, he too feels vindicated by the news. For, by Jim's own lights, his own state of belief is far more valuable than Cliff's.

How can this be? James supplied the answer in his fundamental proposal that one makes a value judgment in trading off the attainment of true belief against the avoidance of error. To continue the story, we can suppose that, like other Impulsives, Jim thinks that individual true beliefs are worth a lot (100 points on the Scale of Doxastic Worth) whereas each false belief is negligible (-1 point on the SDW). Cliff's understanding of the scale is different: he supposes that each false belief is as bad as a true belief is good (they are worth -10 and 10 points, respectively). Jim estimates his own state as worth 9,000 points, Cliff's as worth 999 points; Cliff rates Jim's state at −9,000 points and his own at 90 points. When they talk, Cliff berates Jim for the disaster that his policy of believing things on the basis of insufficient evidence has brought, and there is an initial skirmish about how the term "sufficient evidence" is to be used;[50] but Jim eventually agrees that some (indeed the vast majority) of his beliefs are formed without sufficient evidence when judged by Cliff's standards of sufficiency, protesting that this is a good thing and not the catastrophe Cliff takes it to be. (Their conversation is interrupted by the arrival of two other characters, Blaise and Rene, the former holding that true beliefs have infinite value and false beliefs finite negative value, the latter contending that errors have infinite negative value and true beliefs only finite positive value.)

Plainly, there is something artificial (in fact, downright silly) about the assignments of points that figure in my dramatization of James's insight about the role of value judgments in deciding on standards for inquiry. Not only is it far from obvious that one can atomize systems of belief in the way I have done, but also, more importantly, the value of true or false belief depends crucially on the content of the belief. Yet I think the story is useful in drawing attention to important elements of the dispute between James and Clifford, and when the issues about evaluation are understood more realistically, James's basic thesis is deepened. To assess the merits of Clifford's Principle, one must start with a conception of "sufficient evidence," and here, I suggest, the appropriate understanding is that of evidence that would warrant the community's endorsing a belief as an item of knowledge and inscribing it in the body of lore that is passed on to subsequent generations. A community must have at least implicit standards for judging when the evidence is sufficient (in this sense), it must have norms for fostering (or inhibiting) dissent and questioning the ideas it counts as lore, and it must have norms for permitting (or condemning) individual beliefs that are accepted on grounds that do not satisfy the standards of sufficient evidence. Clifford's Principle is a blanket condemnation of this last type of practice, and, if the arguments of the last section are cogent—or, I think, if the perspectives of both Clifford and James are correct—the principle must be judged in terms of its consequences. That is, it will stand or fall according to whether it figures as part of a system of belief formation and regulation that produces states of the highest expected value, where the value concerned embodies not only our doxastic and epistemic ideals but *all* our ideals. The last section demonstrated, I believe, that the principle fails according to this criterion. But, for both James and Clifford, the crucial question of the permissibility of religious belief is unsettled by that conclusion. We must still inquire whether a practice of permitting the formation of individual religious beliefs, which, *ex hypothesi*, cannot be supported by sufficient evidence, can occur as part of an overall system that meets the consequentialist test as I have just specified it.

Answering that question is plainly going to be difficult, for we are required to consider various alternative ways of embedding practices of individual religious belief in overall social practices and then to evaluate the consequences of each, and we can easily err by not having a sufficiently imaginative view of the realistic possibilities. The strategies pursued by Clifford and by the younger James are easier: Clifford flourishes his principle, and James centers the issue on the idea that his "religious hypothesis" brings potential gain with no possibility of loss. If the arguments I have offered are correct, however, these easy resolutions are inadequate. Instead, both Clifford and James have to proceed by looking for *systematic* effects of religious practice (effects that are likely to remain even when other social practices are modified) that *dominate* among the set of consequences (by having a larger contribution to the overall value). Clifford's essay contains hints about what he would take such effects to be; James's conception of them is elaborated in *Varieties*.

Let us start from the famous division between the "healthy-minded" and the "sick soul." In James's understanding of human temperaments, some people manage to ignore the darker aspects of the world and humanity's role in it, feeling that "Nature, if you will only trust her sufficiently, is absolutely good."[51] His further characterization of this attitude makes it evident that, while it may be charming and attractive, it is also childish and naïve ("It is to be hoped that we all have some friend, perhaps more often feminine than masculine, and young than old, whose soul is of this sky-blue tint, whose affinities are rather with flowers and birds and all enchanting innocencies than with dark human passions, . . . etc.").[52] A later passage makes James's evaluation more explicit:

> To the man actively happy, from whatever cause, evil simply cannot then and there be believed in. He must ignore it; and to the bystander he may then seem perversely to shut his eyes to it and hush it up. But more than this: the hushing of it up may, in a perfectly candid and honest mind, grow into a deliberate religious policy, or *parti pris*.[53]

Here, I suggest, James is preparing the ground for claiming that those who do not feel the human predicament the "sick souls" identify are engaging in some form of therapeutics that involves believing, not only on insufficient evidence but in the teeth of the evidence, that they can ignore certain aspects of reality. He closes his lectures on "The Religion of Healthy-Mindedness" by explicitly considering those who turn to science in adopting this attitude—and there is little doubt that he would regard the Cliffords, the Huxleys, and the Tyndalls of the world as prominent examples—suggesting that this strategy is equivalent to the adoption of religious "mind-cure."[54]

For those who are not born with blind spots to the reality of evil and human finitude, and who do not believe, inevitably on the basis of insufficient evidence, that evil and finitude can be shrugged off or ignored, life must appear bleak. James offers a compelling image:

> Mankind is in a position similar to that of a set of people living on a frozen lake, surrounded by cliffs over which there is no escape, yet knowing that little by little the ice is melting, and the inevitable day drawing near when the last film of it will disappear, and to be drowned ignominiously will be the human creature's portion. The merrier the skating, the warmer and more sparkling the sun by day, and the ruddier the bonfires at night, the more poignant the sadness with which one must take up the meaning of the total situation.[55]

James offers a number of powerful psychological profiles—including Bunyan, Tolstoy, and himself—to show how the sense of human fragility, finitude, and worthlessness affects people whom he views as attuned to their predicament. People of this sort need some belief by which they can live. As James puts it:

> How irrelevantly remote seem all our usual refined optimisms and intellectual and moral consolations in presence of a need of help like this! Here is the real core of the religious problem: Help! help![56]

At this point, the stage is set for showing how various sorts of religious experience (conversions, mystical states, and so forth) serve as valuable responses to this type of predicament. We can now assemble a line of argument that fills out the basic framework of "The Will to Believe" with the detailed exploration of *Varieties*.

It is agreed that we have no way of coming to know religious claims, and the question to be decided is whether it is permissible to believe such claims on the basis of evidence that would not suffice for knowledge. Belief is permissible provided that there is a way of embedding individuals' commitments to religion in a framework of social practices that will produce overall consequences at least as good as those of any alternative that forbids such commitments. The beliefs induced by religious experiences have as a dominant consequence their alleviation of a predicament that the most reflective human beings share, and, indeed, the fruits of endorsing religious experiences typically consist in the transformation of the individual's life in productive ways. Nor can one claim that it is preferable to find an alternative means of coping with the predicament by refusing to accept the reality of the phenomena to which it responds, for that too involves a commitment based upon insufficient evidence, whether it proceeds by endorsing some form of (healthy-minded) religion or by insisting on the completeness of science. Hence, in opposition to Clifford's criticism, religious belief is permissible.

Varieties insists that the predicament for which religion provides treatment is not the idiosyncratic pathology of overly morbid people.[57] In an important discussion, James starts by recognizing that the healthy-minded and the sick souls will characterize each other in unflattering ways.

> To this latter way, the morbid-minded way, as we might call it, healthy-mindedness pure and simple seems unspeakably blind and shallow. To the healthy-minded way, on the other hand, the way of the sick soul seems unmanly and diseased.[58]

This might incline us to think that one of James's indispensable premises (asserting that one cannot find a preferable solution to the predicament by ignoring it) is to be defended by supposing that there is no objective way of deciding between the alternatives he envisages. But he rejects this ecumenical line in favor of a bolder judgment.

> In our own attitude, not yet abandoned, of impartial onlookers, what are we to say of this quarrel? It seems to me that we are bound to say that morbid-mindedness ranges over the wider scale of experience, and that its survey is the one that overlaps . . . even though one be quite free from melancholy one's self, there is no doubt that healthy-mindedness is inadequate as a philosophical doctrine, because the evil facts which it refuses positively to account for are a genuine portion of reality; and they may after all be the best key to life's significance, and possibly the only openers of our eyes to the deepest levels of truth.[59]

It is significant that James's language here foreshadows the description he gives at the very end of the lecture on mysticism, where he tries to sum up his position.[60]

I think the line of argument I have attributed to James is considerably better than anything that the natural reading (or that simple pragmatism) can provide.[61] Yet, in the end, I believe it fails to answer Clifford's challenge. In the final section I shall try to explain why.

VI

Clifford, recall, was concerned that believing things on insufficient evidence would corrupt the intellectual polity and our social arrangements. James has taken the dominant consequence of the adoption of religious experience to lie in the transformation of individual lives, without investigating either how the religious beliefs will affect the advancement of knowledge (individually or collectively) or how those beliefs will be expressed in actions that impinge on others.[62] His brief discussions of these issues suggest that he thinks there are easy ways of dismissing any kindred worries. A first thought is that endorsing religious experience cannot interfere with the pursuit of factual truth.

> As a rule, mystical states merely add a supersensuous meaning to the ordinary outward data of consciousness. They are excitements like the emotions of love or ambition, gifts to our spirit by means of which facts already objectively before us fall into a new expressiveness and make a new connection with our active life. They do not contradict these facts as such, or deny anything that our senses have immediately seized.[63]

The possibility that religious commitments will inspire all kinds of actions, some of which might be socially injurious, is to be handled by reiterating one of the most obvious themes of *Varieties*, the primacy of *individual* religious experience and the downplaying, or outright rejection, of social aspects of religion. In a trenchant critique of the "ecclesiastical spirit," James writes:

> The plain fact is that men's minds are built, as has been often said, in water-tight compartments. Religious after a fashion, they yet have many other things in them besides their religion, and unholy entanglements and associations inevitably obtain. The basenesses so commonly charged to religion's account are thus, almost all of

them, not chargeable at all to religion proper, but rather to religion's wicked practical partner, the spirit of corporate dominion. And the bigotries are most of them in their turn chargeable to religion's wicked intellectual partner, the spirit of dogmatic dominion, the passion for laying down the law in the form of an absolutely closed-in theoretic system.[64]

James's response, then, is that there is nothing to fear from the adoption of religious beliefs (inevitably on insufficient evidence) so long as those beliefs conform to an appropriate set of norms that limit both their content and the ways they may be expressed in action.

It's not hard to envision the kinds of attitudes and actions that perturb Clifford and that James is trying to detach from the permissible endorsement of religious experience. If religious belief leads to adoption of a particular text, read in a particular way, as authoritative, then the factual claims, or presuppositions, of that text may contradict the results of inquiry, conducted scrupulously with proper regard for the evidence—or, perhaps worse, forestall certain lines of inquiry. If religious belief embraces the idea that those who dissent are to be coerced or punished, then, whatever one might think of the value of the transformation effected in the believer, it will hardly be plausible to suppose that the alleviation of the sickness of his soul is the dominant consequence. James's reaction to these threats seems to be to set limits to the ways in which religious experience can affect the subject's doxastic state or her actions, introducing some barrier between private and public comparable to that which I earlier suggested allows for valuable cognitive diversity in the collective practice of inquiry. But the worry is now that the attitudes of the religious believer will have to be so circumscribed, so hedged in by various sorts of norms, that the primacy of religion will be abandoned. Instead of the heroes of *Varieties*, Bunyan and Fox, Tolstoy, St. Francis, and St. Theresa, the ideal religious subject will be some timid ersatz Emersonian, content merely to affirm the existence of the "transcendent."[65] Will any such affirmation alleviate the predicament James so vividly brings before us in *Varieties*? Will it satisfy the "concrete men" whose problem surfaced in "The Will to Believe"?

Even without the heavy weapon of his principle, Clifford can effectively confront James with a dilemma:

Either the adoption of religious belief does make a difference to human judgments and actions, in which case the consequences are likely to be harmful and to outweigh the good effects of the transformation of the life of the individual; or else the adoption is always overridden in practical situations by secular considerations, in which case the belief is empty.

Clifford's dilemma can be made vivid by considering two characters, Faith and Ernest. Ernest treats his religious belief just like anything else of which he feels immediately certain, using it to consider scientific proposals, moral arguments, his possible actions, and so forth. If the belief is thin and insubstantial, a mere gesture toward the "transcendent," then indeed James can claim that Ernest's commitment does not interfere with the pursuit of inquiry or with his moral appraisals and the actions they prompt. If Ernest's belief is substantial, however, then he is committed to giving religious considerations priority in cases of conflict—should he subscribe to a religious doctrine that takes a certain class of people to be evil and therefore to be eliminated, Ernest will pursue them relentlessly, overriding whatever moral principles he would otherwise apply. Faith is different. She always remembers that her religious convictions are founded upon insufficient evidence, and, before appraising new factual ideas or moral questions, she sets her religious convictions on one side, judging matters from the standpoint of evidence and secular moral principle. We might wonder if Faith is even psychologically possible, if the mental compartments to which James confidently alludes are as watertight as that. But, even if she is, it is natural to suggest that her religious belief, like that of the thin and insubstantial version of Ernest, lacks any content. In her case, we find it hard to attribute genuine belief in the pious sentences she mouths, for the doctrines expressed play no role in her doxastic or practical life; in his, the content of belief is nebulous, for there is no connection with further belief formation or with action.

James's version of pragmatism would seem to accord with the assessments just made, and there are several passages in *Varieties* that express similar evaluations. In discussing philosophical attempts to identify and explain the attributes of the deity (aseity, "necessariness," immateriality, and so forth), James invokes "the principle of Peirce, the principle of pragmatism," and asks:

Candidly speaking, how do such qualities as these make any definite connection with our life? And if they severally call for no distinctive adaptations of our conduct, what vital difference can it possibly make to a man's religion whether they be true or false?[66]

The religious commitment cannot be so shackled as it is in the case of Faith, or so insubstantial as it is in the thin version of Ernest. But if James envisages a more robust Ernest, a devout Christian who takes the dicta of the church fathers as authoritative in matters of forming beliefs and coming to action, then Clifford's general reasons for the principle will arise with new force: Ernest's adoption of a belief on the basis of insufficient evidence is a menace to his own clarity of vision, to his own moral practice, and to the well-being of the society in which he lives.[67] James can only evade Clifford's dilemma if he can find a way of embedding Ernest's religious beliefs in a system of norms that prevents the harmful effects, without such complete subordination that made Faith seem a believer in name only.

The heart of the difficulty lies in the fact that, from the perspective of *Varieties*, and indeed from our common understanding of religious commitment, the doctrines of religion take priority. They are supposed to have greater authority than the findings of empirical inquiry or the deliverances of secular morality. Clifford's attempt to defend a general principle succeeds in showing that we can't accept that assignment of authority in situations where there are serious consequences. James's task is to define a sphere within which the traditional authority of religion can be defended, and in which granting that authority will not generate any serious harms.

Once the problem is posed in this way, there's an obvious philosophical precedent, namely Mill's attempt to characterize a private sphere that marks the limits of the law's reach.[68] James cannot simply take over Mill's distinction between public and private, of course, because the issues are importantly different—as can readily be seen by noting that actions in Mill's private sphere are not immune from moral criticism. The task is to find something analogous, the delineation of a range of contexts in which substantive religious belief may direct thought and action, without the subject being vulnerable to Clifford's moral complaint. A first thought is that belief in substantial religious doctrines is morally permissible just in

case the agent adopts norms that militate against the acceptance of that belief, or of any claim whose grounds depend crucially on the belief, as an
item of communitywide knowledge and that prohibit the use of that belief
in decisions that affect the welfare of others. (Here we have something like
an analogue to the insulation of the collective knowledge from individual
belief that I suggested in discussing scientific inquiry in section IV.)

The sphere in which the authority of religion is confined by this proposal is far more limited than that in which religious ideas operate, even
in societies that distinguish between the domains of church and state.
Imagine that Ernest accepts the religious belief that human life is sacred.
As a consequence, he supposes that the use of blastocysts (clusters of em-
bryonic cells at a major developmental stage well before the point at
which the pre-pattern for the nervous system is laid down) to generate
stem cells is prohibited by religion. If Ernest adopts the norms of the last
paragraph, then he must not expect his opinion to carry any weight in
discussions about creating stem cells; indeed, he seems to have an obligation not to voice that opinion. If all Ernest's fellow citizens think as he
does, then their society had better have mechanisms for ensuring that
principles of secular morality are instantiated in public policy, even
though the results run counter to all their "private" views. If Ernest and
his wife Ernestine think alike, and if a routine prenatal test discloses that
the early stage fetus she is carrying has an especially severe genetic condition (San Filippo syndrome, say),[69] then the norms they adopt should
lead them to terminate the pregnancy, for there would otherwise be dele-
terious consequences for others—not only the afflicted child, but also
other members of the family and members of the broader society who
would lose from the diversion of medical and social resources. Of course,
if the society has absorbed Mill's message, there will be no law preventing
the couple from letting the pregnancy continue to term, but the reliance
on religion would be morally wrong, nonetheless.

Yet even though the bounds within which the authority of religion has
been confined are narrow, they are not tight enough. As Clifford saw,
Ernest's belief will play a role in his own intellectual and moral development, possibly preventing him from undertaking inquiries that would
have led him to adopt more refined factual or moral understandings from
those he now has. In consequence, even doing the best he can, there are
likely to be future occasions on which he fails to see things as clearly as he

would otherwise have done, and where that failure to see is costly for others. Effectively, then, Ernest must put his religious commitment on one side in his intellectual and practical explorations and decision making; even in his own thinking, he can't allow himself the luxury of relying on it. Plainly, Ernest, so conceived, is heading asymptotically toward Faith.

James's *Varieties* suggests one—and, I believe, only one—context in which Ernest's religious commitment may permissibly play a role. As we have seen, the heart of the elaboration of his reply to Clifford that James offers in the later work is the delineation of a predicament from which acquiescence in religious belief provides a way out. Let's suppose then that Ernest so confines the authority of his religious belief that its sole effect on his life is to give him a firmly grounded hope that his existence is not pointless and that all will be well. He achieves the benefit James makes central to *Varieties*, but his psychological life is so tightly compartmentalized that there is no spillage into his belief-forming habits or his practical decisions.[70] To almost all intents and purposes, Ernest is the model of a modern secular humanist, differing only in the fact that his strictly leashed religious beliefs are allowed to fill him with hope and serenity. Ernest so conceived satisfies Clifford's strictures. Beyond that, however, Clifford would be right to emphasize the importance of not being earnest.

I doubt that this assessment will bring much consolation to the religious believer, or that it would satisfy James himself. For all the philosophical subtlety of "The Will to Believe" and the argument of *Varieties* that extends it, James succeeds only in defending an exceptionally weak form of religious commitment, secular humanism with a benign gesture. Yet, in my judgment, we should celebrate the works on which I have focused for their scrutiny of the central issues that arise for defenders of religion. In the end, James failed to achieve the defense at which he aimed. But it is no exaggeration to say that nobody who has struggled with that project has ever done better.

NOTES

I am extremely grateful to David Hollinger, Patricia Kitcher, Wayne Proudfoot, Richard Rorty, and Allen Wood for reading a draft of this essay and offering advice, criticisms, and encouragement. Their many valuable suggestions are partially reflected in the final version, but some of the points they raised lead into such rich and interesting issues that much more space would have been required to do their insights and questions justice. In these instances, I have tried to indicate here some lines along which I hope to pursue the discussion in future work.

1. *The Varieties of Religious Experience* (Cambridge: Harvard University Press, 1985), 301. As Wayne Proudfoot reminded me, this conception of James's project is at odds with his own summation in the preface, where he laments that "the unexpected growth of the psychological material" has interfered with his more "metaphysical" plans. That summation underplays the many parts of the text where James is moving on philosophical ground, and plainly offering assessments rather than simple descriptions.

2. Ibid. 301.

3. Ibid.

4. Darwin describes the *Origin of Species* as "one long argument" for his claims about evolution under natural selection. It seems to me that there are many post-Darwinian works that emulate Darwin's strategy of amassing details and showing how they can be systematized; James's *Varieties* is one of them.

5. For a particularly interesting discussion of unconscious psychodynamic causes, see 191; alcohol, nitrous oxide, and ether figure in the treatment of mysticism at 307–308.

6. Ibid. 334, emphasis in original. James has just characterized mystical states in terms of his notions of "twice-bornness," supernaturality, and pantheism. For present purposes, we can ignore the technical details of this characterization and phrase the critical question as one of warranting the truth of claims about transcendent reality.

7. Ibid. 335.

8. This may be too generous to James. If we had neurophysiological probes that revealed a kinship between subjects of religious experience and people who had taken psychotropic drugs, then one might argue that the frequency with which correct beliefs are induced is low (maybe even zero). I take it that some famous observations and experiments in the psychology of religion are crude pointers in this direction. But even with the most refined neurological indicators of similarity, I suspect that the defender of veridical religious experience would continue to insist on some crucial, unmeasured difference. So, for present purposes, I'll be content to claim only that we have no grounds for accepting the reliability of the processes (rather than arguing that we—or our successors—may have grounds for thinking such processes unreliable).

9. James, *Varieties,* 335–336.

10. Although the later sections of this essay will attempt to enlarge the scope of the epistemological discussion by examining James's own ideas, the approach I shall follow will continue to be that of treating James's theses and arguments as if they were advanced in some timeless philosophical discussion. I regard this as *one* fruitful way of approaching his views about religion, but it doesn't exclude other valuable perspectives that locate James in his historical contexts and that

show how the suppleness of his language is sometimes designed to enable his readers to find support for the religious claims that matter to them. In particular, I hope that the project of this essay can form part of a composite picture to which intellectual and social historians and religious scholars (including, most obviously, the authors of other essays in this volume) also contribute.

11. See William James, *Pragmatism* (Cambridge: Harvard University Press, 1975).

12. Ibid. 106. I'm not going to explore James's many intricate discussions of his pragmatist approach to truth; for present purposes, it will be enough to use the slogan as a starting point for arriving at a more adequate account of the strategy of *Varieties*.

13. James, *Varieties,* 335.

14. Ibid. 188.

15. Ibid. 190–191.

16. Ibid. 191.

17. Ibid. 193.

18. See for example the discussions of John Bunyan (154–156), Henry Alline (144–146, 178–180), Stephen Bradley (157–160), S. H. Hadley (166–167), the anonymous "Oxford graduate" (180–183), and the case of Colonel Gardiner ("which everybody may be supposed to know," "cured of sexual temptation in a single hour") (181, 217).

19. Ibid. 210.

20. Ibid. 266.

21. For the quoted phrases, see 299.

22. James maintains that his "test" of religion succeeds "in a general way" and "on the whole" (299); as we have seen, the pragmatist slogan about truth glosses expedience by using the phrases "in almost any fashion," "in the long run," and "on the whole."

23. Ibid. 263.

24. For more extensive discussion of this type of case, see James Griffin, *Well Being* (Oxford: Oxford University Press, 1985) and chapter 13 of my book *The Lives to Come* (New York: Simon & Schuster, 1996).

25. James, *Varieties,* 300. I should note that, here again, as in the earlier posing of the objection (263–265), James only presents the less virulent version of the challenge. In effect, he worries that a religion with humanly *bad* fruits (like "sanguinary sacrifices") might be true. The point that has concerned me is that a religion with what appear to be humanly *good* fruits (consolation, reformation of character) might be false, and that the falsity might undermine the apparent goodness.

26. Ibid. 338.

27. The quoted sentences are from 338–339.

28. Ideally, they should point us both forward and back, to *Pragmatism* and the late writings as well as to "The Will to Believe." I am grateful to both David Hollinger and Wayne Proudfoot for urging me to think about a more extensive

set of connections among James's writings, and I hope to pursue this broader view in a successor to the present essay. For the present, I have tried to ensure that my more limited treatment here is compatible with my present understanding of the broader vision.

29. See James, *Varieties*, Lecture II.

30. Hegel's seminal discussion of the myth of the given was revived in twentieth-century epistemology by Wilfrid Sellars; see "Empiricism and the Philosophy of Mind," in *Science, Perception, and Reality* (London: Routledge, 1963). For elaboration of the argument in the context of religion, see Wayne Proudfoot, *Religious Experience* (Berkeley: University of California Press, 1985).

31. Here I am in general agreement with Charles Taylor, whose book *Varieties of Religion Today* (Cambridge: Harvard University Press, 2002) also connects the discussion of religious experience in *Varieties* to the themes of "The Will to Believe." My reconstruction of James's position and his exchange with Clifford diverges considerably from Taylor's, however, and it seems to me that Taylor's version leaves the central epistemological issues in such soft focus that neither his antipathy to Clifford nor his enthusiasm for James identifies what is interesting and important in either position. Although I don't explicitly contrast my own interpretation with Taylor's, I hope that the discussions of the next sections will do something to substantiate this assessment.

32. W. K. Clifford, "The Ethics of Belief," in *The Ethics of Belief and Other Essays* [reprint] (Amherst, NY: Prometheus Books, 1999), 70–96; I shall cite the generalization as "Clifford's Principle."

33. William James, "The Will to Believe," in *The Will to Believe* (Cambridge: Harvard University Press, 1979), 13–33.

34. Ibid. 15.

35. Here, it seems to me, James should be a model for contemporary philosophy of religion, which, in its current Anglo-American manifestations, typically seems relentlessly committed to Christian apologetics. Very few philosophers seem to appreciate the serious challenge of religious diversity.

36. James, "The Will to Believe," 29. I should note that "more eternal" looks dangerously like a solecism: presumably one thing is more eternal than another if it is closer to being eternal, but the notion of relative closeness to being eternal makes no sense for finite things, all of which are equally distant from (or close to) being eternal in just the way that all finite numbers are equally close to infinity.

37. Ibid. 31.

38. Ibid. 33. It's worth noting that the analogy to the snowbound travelers has to be developed very carefully, since they don't need to come to *believe* that the route they pursue will lead them to safety; instead they act under the belief that *some* action is necessary and the *hope* that *this* action will be successful.

39. Ibid. 32. I should point out that there is a footnote marked in the text after "true," in which James claims an important connection between belief and action, maintaining in particular that if acceptance of the religious hypothesis pro-

duces no difference in action, then "religious faith is a mere superfluity." I shall return to this point below.

40. Clifford, "The Ethics of Belief," 74–77. The medical metaphor is Clifford's own.

41. Peter van Inwagen, "'It is Wrong, Always, Everywhere, and for Anyone to Believe Anything upon Insufficient Evidence'", in *Philosophy and Faith*, ed. David Shatz (New York: McGraw-Hill, 2002), 433–442; Allen Wood, "W. K. Clifford and the Ethics of Belief," in *Unsettling Obligations: Reason, Reality, and the Ethics of Belief* (Stanford: CSLI Publications, 2002).

42. Wood, "W. K. Clifford," 29–32.

43. As Wayne Proudfoot pointed out to me, Clifford* seems to go beyond Clifford in one important respect, for Clifford might claim only that insofar as people form beliefs their beliefs should be true, and might allow that there are good moral reasons for aiding those who suffer rather than pursuing certain kinds of inquiry (a medical researcher, for example, might come to believe that it's more urgent to do clinical work than to continue a line of experiments). But it's easy to see how this version of Clifford could collapse into Clifford*, for, if the claims of suffering humanity are allowed to override the importance of new truth, then it seems that there will be no principled basis for arguing that true beliefs are morally required when false beliefs would bring relief from suffering. But the connections should be explored more thoroughly than space allows here.

44. I have developed an argument along these lines in *Science, Truth, and Democracy* (New York: Oxford University Press, 2001); see especially chapter 6.

45. This case obviously takes the same form of James's examples in which the belief helps to bring about the circumstances that make it true. Sidney Morgenbesser tells me that cases like the one I describe were originally introduced by Roderick Firth. Although I take for granted the possibility of psychosomatic effects, it seems evident that Clifford's Principle can't be seriously defended by denying that possibility. In fact, the case I have described is an idealized version of Stephen Jay Gould's response to his original diagnosis with cancer in the early 1980s. Steve was skeptical about the statistics then available, and his marvelously positive attitude seemed to help him gain twenty more vigorous years. It is very sad that it was only twenty.

46. Allen Wood has suggested to me that the repugnance directed toward Clifford's Principle stems from the conception that that principle will be applied rigidly. Wood wants to maintain that Clifford's Principle is true, but that it should be used judiciously—for, he points out, principles have exceptions ("W. K. Clifford," 38). If I understand him correctly, he thinks that the apparent tension in this position can be resolved by recognizing that we frequently hold as true statements that are only, strictly speaking, approximations to the truth. But, as I have tried to argue elsewhere (in *The Advancement of Science* [New York: Oxford University Press, 1993], 120–124), we make use of the notion of approximate truth in two contexts: one in which we're concerned with ascriptions of numerical magnitude, and

one in which we're interested in generalizations to which there are occasional exceptions. Wood, I believe, thinks of Clifford's Principle as if it were analogous to the former type of case (and to statements like "He weighs 150 pounds" or "The table is flat," statements that we count as true for virtually all practical purposes, but that must be handled carefully in some special, rare contexts); in fact, I think the principle is obviously a case of a generalization, and the point of approximate truth in such instances lies in our inability to specify the conditions under which the generalization fails. Where one can identify a clear set of counterexamples, we don't claim that the generalization is true and that it must be handled judiciously; rather we use our identification to offer a better generalization. One of the achievements of James's essay is that it enables us to do this with respect to Clifford's Principle. So, after James, we no longer need hail Clifford as asserting a true (or "true"?) principle, albeit one that must be applied in a careful (not "rigid") way; we can build the possibility of human consequences that outweigh the benefits of truth into our statement of moral principle. Hence, I don't think that Wood's defense will do, although I must admit that the issues are complex and that I have only indicated the bare lines of argument.

47. See *On Liberty*, section 2 (1859; reprint, Indianapolis: Hackett, 1978), 15–52.

48. For much more detail on the themes of this paragraph, see my essay "The Division of Cognitive Labor," *Journal of Philosophy* 87, 1 (1990): 5–26 and chapter 8 of *The Advancement of Science* (New York: Oxford University Press, 1993). Similar points are made by Robert Merton in his celebrated discussion of the norms of the scientific community, where he points out that the sciences work so well not because individuals behave in accordance with high-minded epistemic principles but because of the norms that govern their interactions ("The Normative Structure of Science," in Robert K. Merton, *The Sociology of Science* [Chicago: University of Chicago Press, 1973], 267–278, especially 276).

49. See his essay cited in note 40.

50. It's a familiar point that Clifford's Principle can be turned into a triviality if one characterizes "sufficient evidence" as that amount of evidence that would release a subject from being blameworthy for adopting the belief. In the story I've told, the Prudent have a conception of sufficient evidence that is elaborated in their educational policies; *perhaps* the Impulsive conceive of sufficient evidence as what their educational system captures, but they may believe that sufficient evidence lies between what they license and the standards adopted by the Prudent, maintaining as well that the other belief-forming practices they allow cover cases in which it is permissible to believe on insufficient evidence.

51. James, *Varieties*, 73. It is worth noting that James credits his famous distinction to Francis W. Newman, from whom he quotes later on this page.

52. Ibid.

53. Ibid. 79.

54. Ibid. 102–105.

55. Ibid. 120.

56. Ibid. 135.

57. Here, it is interesting to compare James with Paul Tillich, who supposes that particular problems arise for human beings at specific stages of our cultural development, with the besetting difficulty for contemporary people arising from our sense of our own meaninglessness. See *The Courage to Be* (New Haven: Yale University Press, 1952).

58. James, *Varieties*, 135.

59. Ibid. 136–137.

60. Ibid. 339; see the passages quoted above on 116–117.

61. It is worth noting that the line of argument I have attributed to James makes the three conclusions of his lecture on mysticism compatible, by interpreting the rights and duties involved in ethical terms. Given (3), and the impossibility of ever settling religious questions by evidence, the subject of mystical states has an ethical right to the beliefs those states produce, while the outsider has no ethical duty to behave likewise. Furthermore, my reconstruction fits with the nascent pragmatism of *Varieties*, again precisely because the religious questions cannot be settled by evidence so that there will be no long-run disadvantage of belief formation because of need for correction.

62. Patricia Kitcher and Richard Rorty have pointed out to me (from slightly different perspectives) that one might also question whether James has succeeded in showing the valuable effects of religion, *construed in his preferred way*, on individual lives. As a preliminary point, we should scrutinize the idea that the cast of reformed characters in *Varieties* constitutes an unbiased sample. More importantly, almost all of James's (or Starbuck's) cases involve people who adopt *substantive* religious views for which they take themselves to have *strong evidence*. These are not reflective agents who make a Jamesian choice among options that they identify as falling beyond the reach of any empirical discoveries. We can only wonder whether clear-headed understanding of the kinds of religion that James views himself as vindicating could work the same transformative effects (and here James's own restless anxieties can provide fuel for doubt). Once again, I am only sketching an issue and a line of argument that deserves more extensive discussion.

63. James, *Varieties*, 338.

64. Ibid. 270–271. See also 294–295.

65. James himself seems clearly to have wanted more than the highly dilute religion I characterize here. As Richard Rorty pointed out to me, that minimal religious commitment fits better the attitudes of James's father, Henry James Sr.

66. James, *Varieties*, 352. I find similar attitudes expressed, less forthrightly, at 39 and 66. James's castigation of scholasticism seems to me to be fundamentally right, and to apply to many contemporary exercises in the philosophy of religion. As mentioned above (note 39), there is also a strong statement of the theme in a footnote in James, "The Will to Believe," 32.

67. Here I am in agreement with Wood, who gives eloquent expression to an important point: "To people who don't get it about Clifford's Principle, the evils

that result directly from its violation do not usually seem serious. They usually think of the kinds of religious beliefs that are mixed with such insipid or saccharine sentiments that it seems hard to see how they could do harm, forgetting about cases such as Clifford's shipowner, as well as about the fact that many religious beliefs, when people get serious about them, are not so nice" ("W. K. Clifford," 35).

68. J. S. Mill, *On Liberty*.

69. I choose this example because it involves developmental disruption, pain for the child, and high levels of hostility and aggression.

70. I concede the psychological possibility of this version of Ernest. If that concession is wrong, then James's defense is even more problematic.